AMERICAN LEGACY
Our National Forests

COLORADO'S WHITE RIVER NATIONAL FOREST, CARR CLIFTON/MINDEN PICTURES; SPRIG OF LODEGEPOLE PINE, LYLE ROSBOTHAM (PAGE 1)

BY KENNETH BROWER

. . . .

Prepared by the Book Division
National Geographic Society
Washington, D.C.

AMERICAN LEGACY Our National Forests

By Kenneth Brower

Featuring photographs by Raymond Gehman

PUBLISHED BY THE NATIONAL GEOGRAPHIC SOCIETY

Reg Murphy, *President and Chief Executive Officer*
Gilbert M. Grosvenor, *Chairman of the Board*
Nina D. Hoffman, *Senior Vice President*

PREPARED BY THE BOOK DIVISION

William R. Gray, *Vice President and Director*
Charles Kogod, *Assistant Director*
Barbara A. Payne, *Editorial Director*

STAFF FOR THIS BOOK

Tom Melham, *Managing Editor*
Greta Arnold, *Illustrations Editor*
Lyle Rosbotham, *Art Director*

REDBUDS ABLOOM IN MERCED RIVER CANYON OF CALIFORNIA'S SIERRA NATIONAL FOREST, BRENDA THARP

Bonnie S. Lawrence, Kimberly A. Kostyal, Elisabeth B. Booz, *Researchers*

Harvey Arden, Gary Soucie, John Thompson, *Picture Legend Writers*

Carl Mehler, *Map Editor*

Thomas L. Gray, *Map Researcher*

Lewis R. Bassford, *Production Project Manager*

Richard S. Wain, *Production*

Meredith C. Wilcox, *Illustrations Assistant*

Kevin G. Craig, Dale-Marie Herring, Peggy J. Purdy, *Staff Assistants*

MANUFACTURING AND QUALITY CONTROL
George V. White, *Director*

John T. Dunn, *Associate Director*

Vincent P. Ryan, *Manager*

Polly P. Tompkins, *Executive Assistant*

Elisabeth MacRae-Bobynskyj, *Indexer*

Library of Congress CIP Data: page 200

CONTENTS

SUNRISE IN BOUNDARY WATERS CANOE AREA WILDERNESS OF MINNESOTA'S SUPERIOR NATIONAL FOREST, RAYMOND GEHMAN

ALASKA

Anchorage•

CHUGACH

U.S.
CANADA

TONGASS

Juneau•

TONGASS

0   300 mi

0   300 km

OLYMPIC

Seattle•   MT.
              BAKER-
              SNOQUALMIE

OKANOGAN   COLVILLE

WENATCHEE   KANIKSU   KOOTENAI

                              LEWIS
GIFFORD   COEUR   AND
PINCHOT   WASHINGTON   D'ALENE   CLARK

Portland•   ST. JOE   LOLO

MT.   CLEARWATER   LOLO   MONTANA
HOOD   UMATILLA
SIUSLAW   NEZ   HELENA   NORTH
       CROOKED   UMATILLA   PERCE   DAKOTA
       RIVER   WALLOWA-   DEERLODGE   LEWIS AND CLARK
WILLAMETTE   OCHOCO   WHITMAN   BITTERROOT   LITTLE
                PAYETTE   BEAVERHEAD   MISSOURI
              OREGON   MALHEUR   GALLATIN   CEDAR
UMPQUA   DESCHUTES   OCHOCO   SALMON   CUSTER   CUSTER   RIVER   SHEYENNE
       ROGUE   AND
SISKIYOU   RIVER   CHALLIS   TARGHEE   CUSTER   GRAND RIVER
       WINEMA   FREMONT   BIGHORN   SOUTH
KLAMATH   BUTTE VALLEY   SHOSHONE   DAKOTA
SIX   BOISE   SAWTOOTH   BLACK
RIVERS   MODOC   IDAHO   THUNDER   HILLS
SHASTA-   SAWTOOTH   CARIBOU   BRIDGER-   BASIN   FORT
TRINITY   HUMBOLDT   TETON   BUFFALO   PIERRE
LASSEN   CURLEW   WYOMING   GAP
                        WASATCH-   OGLALA   SAMUEL R.
MENDOCINO   CACHE   MEDICINE   NEBRASKA   McKELVIE
PLUMAS   NEVADA   HUMBOLDT   BOW
TAHOE   HUMBOLDT   Salt Lake City•   MEDICINE BOW   NEBRASKA   NEBRASKA
ELDORADO   WASATCH-   ASHLEY
       TOIYABE   CACHE   UINTA   ROUTT   PAWNEE
San   HUMBOLDT   ASHLEY   ROOSEVELT
Francisco•   STANISLAUS   FISHLAKE   MANTI-LA SAL   ARAPAHO   •Denver
       TOIYABE   UTAH   WHITE   KANSAS
SIERRA   INYO   GRAND   RIVER   PIKE
CALIFORNIA   HUMBOLDT   MESA   COLORADO
LOS   SEQUOIA   INYO   FISHLAKE   UNCOMPAHGRE   GUNNISON   SAN
PADRES   ISABEL
SEQUOIA   TOIYABE   DIXIE   MANTI-   RIO
                        LA SAL   SAN JUAN   GRANDE   SAN
LOS   ISABEL
PADRES   KAIBAB   CARSON   COMANCHE   CIMARRON
ANGELES   KAIBAB   CARSON
Los Angeles•   SAN   PRESCOTT   COCONINO   CIBOLA   SANTA FE   KIOWA   RITA
       BERNARDINO   BLANCA   OKLA.
CLEVELAND   ARIZONA   APACHE-   Albuquerque•   CIBOLA   BLACK
San Diego•   Phoenix•   SITGREAVES   KETTLE   Oklahoma•
                TONTO   NEW MEXICO   McCLELLAN   City
                    GILA   CIBOLA   CIBOLA   CREEK
                MEXICO   LINCOLN
                    CORONADO   LINCOLN   LYNDON B. JOHNSON
                                    LINCOLN   TEXAS
                        El Paso•

CANADA

0   400 mi

0   400 km

San Antonio•

National Forest

National Forest Boundary

National Grassland

AMERICAN LEGACY
Our National Forests

PUERTO RICO

San Juan

CARIBBEAN

Scale same as main map

The Legacy

. . . .

If you were to graph the worldwide increase in human population since the beginnings of history, you'd wind up with a mirror image of the curve for the global decline of forests. The Fertile Crescent that embraced ancient Mesopotamia—a key cradle of civilization—actually *was* fertile once, its hilly watershed protected by primeval cedar forest. *The Epic of Gilgamesh*, a Sumerian classic recorded on 12 clay tablets at Nineveh, is an allegory for how all this changed. It tells how Gilgamesh, ruler of the Mesopotamian city-state of Uruk, determined to immortalize himself by making his city grand. To build he needed timber. None before him had ever had the hubris to enter the cedar forest, for Enlil, the supreme Sumerian deity, had assigned the fierce demigod Humbaba to guard the trees. Tribal taboos and supernatural guardians then were commonplace throughout the planet; such beliefs helped conserve natural resources. Gilgamesh's breakthrough was in his disdain for such cautionary tales. In that sense he was ahead of his time, a truly modern man.

About 4,700 years ago—when today's oldest bristlecone pines were only seedlings—Gilgamesh and his axmen entered the cedar forest. They hesitated, swayed briefly by the beauty of the trees. Coming to himself, Gilgamesh gave the order; his men set about felling cedars. Humbaba confronted them and ordered them from the forest, but they stood their ground. (Although Humbaba was half a god, Gilgamesh was two-thirds divine.) Battle was joined. Humbaba was defeated and beheaded. The cedars moaned in the wind, and the army of axmen resumed their chopping unhindered.

Over time, the tapestry of cedar forest began to unravel. Gilgamesh's depredations were followed by those of Gudea, king of nearby Lagash, then by those of the Third Dynasty at Ur. The Bronze Age arrived and, with it, increasing demands for wood to fuel foundry fires, to build palaces and homes, and to furnish and decorate living spaces. Deforested hillsides eroded; Mesopotamia's rivers ran cloudy; silt clogged the area's marvelously

MICHIGAN DEPARTMENT OF NATURAL RESOURCES

Overcut by logging, undercut by erosion, stumps in this old Michigan clear-cut seem to tiptoe toward oblivion. Just over a century ago, growing awareness of such wanton misuse of America's resources sparked a bold new vision: the national forest idea.

engineered irrigation canals. By 2000 B.C., wood was so scarce in Babylon that rental houses had no doors—tenants had to carry their own from house to house. Mineral salts, washing down from sedimentary rock exposed by deforestation, were accumulating in the fields. The Fertile Crescent was no longer so fertile. Crops failed, yields fell, great Sumerian cities declined into villages or vanished entirely. Today, Mesopotamia— cradle of civilization, core of the Fertile Crescent, site of the Garden of Eden, birthplace of the wheel—is the sandy desert where Saddam Hussein, the latest incarnation of Gilgamesh, maneuvers his tanks.

The mountains of Phoenicia were green once, covered thickly by the cedars of Lebanon. This forest, more than a million acres in extent, provided wood for a succession of empires. An inscription on Egypt's Temple of Karnak records the arrival some 5,000 years ago of 40 Phoenician ships laden with Lebanon cedar. Two thousand years later, enough trees remained for Hiram, King of Tyre, to promise King Solomon sufficient cypress and cedar for construction of the temple at Jerusalem. Solomon is supposed to have sent 80,000 axmen to work the forest and 70,000 skidders to roll the logs to sea. Some 500 years after this Solomonic invasion, there were *still* cedars left, remarkably, and they helped fuel the megalomania of Babylon's most notorious king, Nebuchadnezzar. "Magnificent palaces and temples I have built," he boasted. "Huge cedars from Mount Lebanon I cut down. With radiant gold I overlaid them and with jewels I adorned them." Lebanon's cedars could not sustain all this Ozymandian ambition forever, and today they survive only in a few small groves.

Mycenaean Greece, the Greece of Homer's *Iliad*, also was covered by extensive forests that declined with the economic boom of the Late Bronze Age, the trees feeding foundries, kilns, and cooking fires. Forests were logged, soils eroded, and boom turned to crash. Towns died; cities decayed. By the 11th century B.C., the end of the Mycenaean Period, Greece had lost 75 percent of its population. The authors of the Greek epic *Cypria* understood the Malthusian dynamic that overtook them (long before Thomas Malthus would contemplate it). Human numbers and human greed, they wrote, "oppressed the surface of the deep-bosomed earth." Zeus, surveying this wounded land, initiated the Trojan War "so that the load of death might empty the world."

By the fifth century B.C. all Attica had been deforested. Plato, for one, was stunned by the speed of the decline. In his *Critias* he lamented that Attica's soil had recently been deep, the forests thick. "What now remains of what then existed is like the skeleton of a sick man, all the fat and soft earth wasted away." Rome, too, began amid forest. The first Romans were a sylvan people. But by the time of Christ, the very species of tree that had framed Roman civilization—lowland fir—no longer grew in the lowlands. It occurred only "high up on the mountains," wrote Pliny, "as though it had run away from the sea."

So it went in all cradles of civilization. Cities went up, forests came down; in time the cities died and crumbled. Cyprus was deforested, and Crete, and Syria. Carthage was deforested—then the rest of North Africa. The great forests that once covered much of India receded into scattered islands of trees. China's forests also fell, and in no cradle were the devastating impacts of deforestation more complete. The great earthen dikes that even now contain the Yellow River, elevating its channel as much as 50 feet above the plain of its delta, are monuments to the determination of millions of peasants over four millennia. They also memorialize the ruthless efficiency of ancient Chinese loggers, for the Yellow River's namesake color stems from silts washed down its vast and deforested watershed.

The first European explorers and colonists to reach the New World saw what ancient Phoenicians, Carthaginians, Greeks, Romans, and Chinese had all seen much earlier: forests that seemed endless and inexhaustible. In 1492, Christopher Columbus reported that the interior mountains of Hispaniola were "accessible and filled with trees of a thousand kinds and tall. I am told they never lose their foliage, as I can understand, for I saw them as green and lovely as they are in Spain in May."

Today very little of Hispaniola's original cover remains. The western third of this island is Haiti, once France's richest New World colony, a former cornucopia of sugar, indigo, cotton, cacao, and coffee grown on hills relentlessly cleared of trees. It is now a destitute and broken land.

On the Atlantic coast of South America, Portuguese axes cut into trees the Tupi Indians called *ibirapitanga*, or "red tree." At first cut, the wood shows a golden core. Then it turns bright orange-red, and after immersion in water, reddish violet. The Portuguese christened it *pau-brasil*—glowing coal—and their king named his vast American colony for it. In trade for steel axes, the Tupi brought out tons of ibirapitanga logs, initiating the decline of Brazil's great Atlantic forest, some 250 million acres of coastal woodland that is now almost entirely gone—one of the most endangered forests on earth. Meanwhile, on that continent's Pacific coast, Spanish axes cut into ancient groves of *alerce*, the giant conifer of Patagonia's temperate rain forest, a southern analogue of California's redwood. In North America, the birch, maple, hemlock, and beech forests of the Northeast fell, then the southern woods. Loggers reached the Great Lakes by 1830 and began felling that region's lofty white and red pines. History was repeating itself one more time.

But then something new happened. As the American frontier began to close in the middle of the 19th century, a group of thinkers, artists, writers, and scientists had a collective vision. They sensed history repeating itself and foresaw the end of America's forests.

The idea of setting aside forest was not original with them. Aristotle considered conservation a state obligation, proposing that Athens appoint magistrates to watch over its forests. Cicero railed in the Roman senate against the sale of state-owned forest to private industry—the sort of sweetheart deal that has plagued forestry for ages. Even North America's earliest colonists realized the forest's potential for abuse. As early as 1626—just six years after the *Mayflower* landed—residents of Plymouth, Massachusetts, passed ordinances regulating timber-cutting. In 1681, William Penn decreed that for every five acres cleared in the colony of Pennsylvania, one acre should be kept forested. (Pennsylvania means "Penn's Forest," after all.) Among later generations of Americans, a kind of murmur grew. Thoreau and Emerson chimed in with their writings; Audubon, Mark Catesby, and William Bartram with their art. For whatever reasons, conservation took root in American soil as it never had before.

FRED HIRSCHMANN

Winter finery graces trees and spires of Wyoming's otherworldly Wind River Range within Shoshone National Forest. Abutting Yellowstone National Park, this first of our national forests was set aside in 1891, following passage of the Forest Reserve Act.

Perhaps it grew from the realization that the Americas were the last New World on earth. Perhaps it involved the speed at which our forests were vanishing. (The cedars of Lebanon had lasted millennia under the ax. North America's white pines were going in decades.) Perhaps it stemmed in part from the nature of American democracy. We have our little Gilgameshes and Nebuchadnezzars, but we are not ruled despotically by big ones. Surely the flowering of this nation's conservation movement also had a lot to do with luck and the fact that much of the West was still forested.

When George Perkins Marsh published his epochal *Man and Nature* in 1864, the conservation movement had found its focus and its philosopher. Marsh was a Vermonter, also a politician, scientist, diplomat, and linguist. As a young man, curious about erratic streamflow through his home town of Woodstock, he had traced the problem to deforestation and overgrazing of hills above town. Taking that lesson with him as the U.S. minister to Turkey, he saw that the ruin of the eastern Mediterranean's oldest civilizations clearly had begun with deforestation. He returned to find the New England forests of his boyhood almost entirely gone. "We have now felled forest enough everywhere, in many districts far too much," he wrote. "Let us restore this one element of material life to its normal proportions, and devise means for maintaining the permanence of its relations to the fields, the meadows, and the pastures, to the rain and the dews of heaven, to the springs and rivulets with which it waters the earth."

The census of 1890 shocked the American psyche, for it announced the closing of the frontier; here was an official end to any illusion that more forest would always lie beyond the horizon. On October 1, 1890, Congress set aside more than 1,500 square miles of the Sierra Nevada as "reserved forest lands." Five months later it passed the Forest Reserve Act, which empowered the President to proclaim forest reserves on the nation's public lands. Only three weeks after that, on March 30, 1891, President Benjamin Harrison established, adjacent to Yellowstone National Park, the Yellowstone Park Timber Land Reserve, one and a quarter million acres of trees that are now part of Shoshone National Forest. Grover Cleveland added nearly 26 million acres to the forest reserves. William McKinley was responsible for 7 million more. Theodore Roosevelt began cautiously in his first term then let himself go, by the end of his second term more than tripling the size of the nation's forest reserve system, to 151 million acres.

Eastern states, initially, were not greatly affected by the Forest Reserve Act, since most lands there already were in private hands; little remained within the public domain. But by 1911, severe flooding resulting from overcutting of Eastern watersheds induced Congress to pass the Weeks Act, which provided for the purchase of "forested, cut-over or denuded lands within the watersheds of navigable streams"—and helped initiate the creation of national forests in the East.

The first great age in American conservation came, then, around the turn of the century. A deep and abiding schism in the movement opened at the same time. The rift is personified by two of the movement's leaders, Gifford Pinchot and John Muir. In 1892, John Muir founded the Sierra

Club—the same year that Gifford Pinchot introduced German forestry practices to the battered forests of North Carolina. Pinchot soon would become chief of the federal Division of Forestry, a forerunner of the National Forest Service. He and Muir began as friends and allies but had a falling-out over core beliefs. Muir's passion was nature, Pinchot's was natural resources. Muir was preoccupied with the spiritual, Pinchot with the utilitarian. "The object of our forest policy is not to preserve the forests because they are beautiful, or because they are refuges for wild creatures," Pinchot wrote. The object was "the making of prosperous homes. Every other concern comes as secondary."

Pinchot took upon himself and his school of thought the mantle "conservationist." Muir and others became "preservationists." There has never been parity between the two schools. Pinchot's philosophy would come to dominate government agencies like the Bureau of Land Management, the Fish and Wildlife Service, and the modern Forest Service—now part of the federal Department of Agriculture. Muir's philosophy finds support in the National Park Service and has inspired nongovernmental organizations such as the Sierra Club and the Wilderness Society. The armies of Muir have established various beachheads, especially in the last half of this century, but Pinchot's army still holds most of the terrain. Much of the debate over national forests today can be seen as a continuing argument between the vociferous ghosts of these two men.

It was winter, the off-season, when I drove into Pisgah National Forest, North Carolina, the first national forest created in the East. Preservation of cultural sites is one of the obligations of the modern Forest Service, and in Pisgah's Cradle of Forestry, a national historic site, the agency has preserved a fossil seed of itself.

That seed was planted in 1889 by the millionaire George Vanderbilt, who began buying up logged and farmed-over land around Asheville, North Carolina, in hopes of establishing an estate where forest would be managed sensibly. He called it Pisgah Forest, after a local mountain named for the biblical Mount Pisgah, from which Moses saw the promised land. Vanderbilt invited Frederick Law Olmsted, the nation's most famous designer of parks, to landscape part of it. Olmsted recommended Gifford Pinchot as forester for the entire estate, and in fact Pinchot spent some time here, testing his ideas. He was succeeded by Dr. Carl Schenck, a

German forester who set up on Vanderbilt's estate the first forestry school in the U.S. The Cradle of Forestry celebrates this pioneer institution.

I walked Campus Trail, a mile-long path connecting the old buildings of Schenck's school. Every spring and summer the past comes alive here as weavers, spinners, quilters, woodsmen, blacksmiths, and others demonstrate turn-of-the-century Appalachian arts. Now the trail was quiet; amid bare hardwoods and scattered hemlocks and rhododendrons, the school

PAT O'HARA

Rhododendrons blush shamelessly along Cloudland Trail in Pisgah National Forest, North Carolina. Home to the Cradle of Forestry, Pisgah includes 80,000 acres once owned by the Vanderbilts and managed, briefly, by a young and ambitious forester named Gifford Pinchot.

had aged gracefully. Gray, weathered shingles capped Schenck's schoolhouse and commissary, as well as the barn he had used for an office. Some walls were still chinked with red clay, accented by a string of red peppers someone had hung on a porch.

A skeleton staff at the visitor center tried to warm up the theater for me, but the heater balked. I zipped up my jacket, alone amid all the rows of seats, and watched a dreary little documentary rendered in classic visitor-center style: bad prose and tinny flute music. The soundtrack was raspy, the color weary—no doubt from countless screenings throughout previous summers. At least half the budget for this film, it seemed to me, had gone into the enormous, waxed, upturned black mustaches worn by the amateur actor playing Carl Schenck. I found myself objecting almost immediately to the script.

"If a forest is to be healthy, it needs the wisdom of a seasoned forester," the narrator said.

I laughed aloud. The planet's woodlands, according to this dictum, had been unhealthy from their beginnings, in the Devonian forests of 365 million years ago. Forests had been diseased and decrepit until the arrival of foresters. The poor trees. How had they ever muddled through? The film then described Schenck's arrival in America. Emigrating from Germany with a degree in forestry, he encountered a strange land, strange language, and strange culture; "a challenge he met with typical Prussian determination," the narrator said. The actor playing Schenck—after delivering a prologue in an accent too thick for me to decipher—declaimed, "These misshapen trees must go, to give new shoots a chance."

"Yes," I muttered. "*Nazi* forestry."

This was unfair to Schenck, of course—he had been a decent man who contributed many sensible principles to American forestry. But there was no one in the theater to hear, and there was a germ of accuracy in my words. God does not make misshapen trees. Schenck's contemporary, the poet Joyce Kilmer, who has a memorial grove in Nantahala National Forest adjacent to Pisgah, could have told him that. Forestry that imposes some sort of ideal of tree form is not enlightened forestry.

If it is not obvious yet, then I should state that, in the great Pinchot-Muir debate, I am a Muirian. It's in the blood. I am a son of David Brower, first executive director of the Sierra Club, who in the 1950s and 1960s led that organization into its second flowering. I was *reared* in the army of Muir.

Gifford Pinchot, there is no denying, is a hero of the conservation movement. Without his influence on Teddy Roosevelt, today's national forests would almost surely have been much smaller. Pinchot's efficient and semi-scientific forestry was immensely superior to the wasteful, short-sighted logging that had devastated the East and was moving steadily west. But it also is true that by adamantly advocating the utilitarian, Pinchot effectively hijacked American forestry from thinkers like George Perkins Marsh, who held practical and aesthetic concerns in better balance. Pinchot was a man with large and yet limited vision. By the end of the film I remained unconvinced that he, from this Pisgah, had truly seen the promised land.

Three months after my visit to the Cradle of Forestry, I was some 1,600 miles away in eastern Arizona, waking under a thin canopy of mesquite, at the edge of the Sierra Ancha Wilderness of Tonto National Forest. The mesquite was in its spring bloom of yellow catkins, beautiful against the pale dawn sky. Gambel's quail were clucking and chortling somewhere uphill, under farther mesquites. My son David, curled up fetally in his sleep-

ing bag, had rolled up against me in the night, as usual. He weighs about a third of what I do, yet somehow, as always, he had managed to push me and my bag halfway off the ground cloth. I tweaked him awake. We had breakfast with photographer Raymond Gehman and our guides, Linda Sullivan of the Forest Service and her son Levi, then filled our canteens and put out the campfire. Hoisting day packs, we headed up Cold Springs Canyon toward the otherwise nameless cliff dwelling that archaeologists have designated "Arizona C:1:36."

Top-hatted President Theodore Roosevelt and Gifford Pinchot—first chief forester of the Forest Service— worked tirelessly to expand our national forests. T.R.'s 1901-1909 administration added about 100 million acres to the system, more than tripling its size.

Not all cultural legacies in our national forests are historical; many are prehistoric. My fieldwork for this book has taken me to a good deal of America's pre-Columbian antiquity. Take, for example, the Sewee Shell Rings of Francis Marion National Forest: Deep middens of oyster and clam shells discarded by generations of South Carolina Indians who began shucking some 5,000 years ago— about the time that the shipment of Phoenician cedar described on the Temple of Karnak arrived in Egypt. Then there's the Medicine Wheel of Wyoming's Big Horn National Forest, its 28 radiating spokes of stone perhaps serving its builders as some sort of astronomical observatory, if speculation is correct. Arizona C:1:36 was to be another stop on this tour of ancient places.

Levi and David led the way up through blackjack oaks, Arizona cypress, mesquite, agave, cholla, and prickly pear. The canyon was inordinately dry even for this land of little rain; the Southwest was in the throes of its worst drought in 80 years. Still, some cactuses were in flower, and a few lupine, and all the mesquite. The terrain steepened. In several places the path was all loose dirt and scree; we had to grip trees and shrubs to haul ourselves up. We cursed the cliff dwellers jovially and agreed that they must have been crazy to have made this trip daily, leaving the cliffs for their gardens on the canyon floor, then climbing home again. Such a lifestyle testified to endurance, surefootedness, and a tremendous fear of something.

Arizona C:1:36 is a beautiful little ruin. The entrance is fortress-like. Its ancient builders, on finding a vertical cleft they liked—one of those shafts that rock climbers call a chimney—had chocked it side-to-side with a bulwark of flat sandstone slabs that seemed almost animate, as if they had willed themselves into place. Both the stones and the mud mortar were of warm desert colors. It was wonderful how the builders had fitted the slabs to the irregularities of the cleft, which narrowed as it went up. Their architecture harmonized with the desert as no modern architecture harmonizes with its landscape. Perfect rectilinearity does not exist in nature, nor in the cities of America's cliff dwellers.

Entry was through a window high on the wall. Levi and David, aged 13 and 10, were about the size of the adult Indians who had built this place. They climbed up nimbly. We three grown-ups followed more ponderously. The masonry was 700 years old yet felt remarkably solid. Squeezing in through the window, I found myself in a small antechamber from which a log pole led up toward two stories of rooms above. In places the mud floors dividing upper rooms from lower were still intact, and they had a timbrous resonance underfoot. The mud of the floors and mortar of the walls were textured everywhere with impressions of smallish fingers—the final touches of the masons, recorded for eternity. The deep shadow of the cleft was blessedly cool after the hot scramble of the climb. Soot from generations of cooking fires still blackened the ceiling, deepening the pleasant midday twilight inside the cave.

It was not a big ruin, like Mesa Verde or Chaco Canyon, but for the moment it was ours. No marked trail led to it. No 20th-century Caucasian or Navajo had invented some apocryphal name for it. No signs warned us off fragile sections, no self-guiding booklets referred to stenciled numbers beneath this kiva or that granary. Any interpretation would be our own.

The innermost rooms gave way to a short stretch of narrow, natural cavern, then a dogleg turn opened onto a somewhat wider cave, which had been divided into rooms and ended in a wedge of bright light—a rock window, opening onto the canyon's sun-drenched wall. An archaeologist who surveyed this ruin in the 1930s had called the opening "the Look-out"; it looked straight down an unscalable cliff. Cool, persistent drafts wafted through the cave, blowing especially strong and refreshing at the dogleg. Linda Sullivan paused there, clearly enjoying it, like an office worker before a fan. She suggested that maybe the original inhabitants of these cliffs had come not out of fear but for the natural air-conditioning. It seemed as good an explanation as any.

The building of these dwellings began about 1278, a time when the cliff-adapted civilization to the north— the Anasazi culture of the Four Corners area—was dying. Why did a sudden burst of construction occur here even as it ceased there? Sierra Ancha's builders always sought places like this one, inaccessible and out-of-the-way. Some archaeologists have suggested that such outposts were less villages and more timber camps inhabited by prehistoric loggers. For 70 years these

RAYMOND GEHMAN

Exploring prehistory in the Sierra Ancha Wilderness of Arizona's Tonto National Forest, author Kenneth Brower and his son David clamber through the draft-cooled chambers of Arizona C:1:36, a cliff dwelling abandoned by its builders around 1350.

cliffs were occupied; then, around 1350, the entire region was abandoned. The next people to arrive in Sierra Ancha were nomadic speakers of Athapascan—the legendary Apaches.

No one knows why the ancients vanished. In the cool cleft of Arizona C:1:36, I sat and pondered. Plague, perhaps? In 1350, when Sierra Ancha was being abandoned, the Black Death was reaching its climax in Europe. Something similar might have ravaged these people. One hypothesis suggests they were displaced by fiercer tribes, but this view has been long out of favor. Tree-ring evidence points to a prolonged, 20-year drought at the time of abandonment, a great desiccation compared to our little drought of the moment. Current consensus among the experts is that the failure of both the Anasazi and Mogollon civilizations lay in those two decades of failed rains.

I thought again about my visit to Pisgah National Forest's Cradle of Forestry. That historical site had not filled me with patriotism and enthusiasm for national forests. What had were prehistoric places like Arizona C:1:36. That very afternoon, bushwhacking through mountain mahogany, we would find another ancient cliff dwelling. The American Southwest, too, was a cradle. Tens of thousands of sites, many still unexcavated, are scattered throughout Four Corners country; so many, indeed, that I have sometimes wondered: Could the inhabitants, by their very numbers, have contributed to their own demise? Did these cliff dwellers overwhelm their landscape—much as the inhabitants of the Fertile Crescent overwhelmed their ancient forests?

The lost cities and towns of the New World's deserts bear haunting resemblance to those of the Old. In each, ruined walls and empty towers of warm-hued stone rest amid dry landscapes carved by the wind. There the vanished cultures were Sumerian, Babylonian, Syrian, Carthaginian. Here they were Hohokam, Mogollon, Sinagua, Mimbres, Anasazi. A biblical lesson seems to reside in them all. They remind us that civilizations come and go; that greenness waxes but mostly wanes as mankind advances. They are an admonition that any civilization, wherever it happens to arise, is dependent in the end on its soil, its water, and its trees. 🌰

Timeless graffiti of petroglyphs from the long-vanished Southern Sinagua culture adorn a cliff in Arizona's Coconino National Forest, south of Grand Canyon. Animal figures suggest a greener, less desertified environment than today's.

FOLLOWING PAGES: Gorgeously arthritic forest Methuselah, an ancient bristlecone pine stands sentry over the millennia in Inyo National Forest, eastern California. Individuals of this species have lived more than 4,700 years.

Clouds to daydream by
drift like idle thoughts
above Idaho's Sawtooth
National Forest. Seeking
to balance wilderness
preservation with wisely
managed use of its many
natural resources, our
national forest system
also holds out a tacit
promise: That each and
every visitor can find
herein an acre of quietude
and a harvest of serenity.

FOLLOWING PAGES:
Beyond a foreground of
blooming fireweed,
iridescent algae give a
glowing, satiny sheen to
mudflats at the foot of the
Chugach Mountains, in
southern Alaska's
Chugach National Forest.

JACK DYKINGA

Just a stone's throw from eternity, boulders within West Cochise Stronghold strike a precarious balance for the ages in Arizona's Coronado National Forest. Similarly remote desert redoubts sheltered the renegade Apache chief Cochise as he repeatedly eluded thousands of pursuing U.S. troops during the 1860s.

Green with algae, sandstone cliffs such as these occur in the more humid areas of Kentucky's Red River Gorge, part of Daniel Boone National Forest.

FOLLOWING PAGES: *Mountains roll like ocean breakers across Washington State's Olympic National Forest, which includes temperate rain forest.*

PRECEDING PAGES: *Rising from the ruins of day-long rainstorms, a flaming summer's evening gutters out in the waters of Island River, near the western tip of Lake Superior in northern Minnesota's Superior National Forest.*

"Shrieking vitriol blue," peripatetic naturalist John Muir described Alaska's wondrously hued glacial ice (left), seen here in Tongass National Forest. Compacted over time by their cumulative weight, ice crystals absorb reds and yellows of the spectrum, reflecting to the eye blues of astonishing intensity.

FOLLOWING PAGES: *Rivaling an Impressionist masterpiece, sugar maples dappled by autumn take on an intensity all their own, in Vermont's Green Mountain National Forest.*

Of Forests and Trees

Today our system of national forests includes 20 grasslands as well as 155 forests, for the mandate of the U.S. Forest Service (USFS) has grown to include vast regions of prairie and sagebrush as well as trees. Together, all agency reserves cover 191.6 million acres, an area nearly the size of the states of Washington, Oregon, and California, combined. Happily, they are *not* combined but scattered; in their far-flungness they provide a nearly complete cross-section of America's highly varied ecosystems. Stewardship by the USFS has been spotty: spectacular successes early, then some egregious failures of the public trust. Even so, the system of national forestlands that we have inherited continues to surpass any other on earth. Somehow, the national parks have acquired most of the glamour associated with America's public domain. It is easy to take our forests for granted, and I have done so often myself.

Returning recently from the tropical rain forest of the Peruvian Amazon, I found myself heading off only three weeks later for the temperate rain forest of the Pacific Northwest—an area I knew from my childhood. The Amazon was still very much with me, however: The commotion of its spider monkeys and the motionlessness of its sloths; the windy roar of its howler monkeys and the rude, Bronx-cheery blows of its river dolphins; the pet marmosets worn like berets in the black hair of Indian girls; the warning chatter and iridescent blues and greens of Amazon kingfishers darting low over the river; the raucous screams and brilliant plumage of scarlet macaws soaring high above.

Rain forests are always greener on the other side of the Equator. The exotic, as a rule, is more wonderful than the familiar. So it was that the nearer I got to Washington State's Olympic Peninsula and Olympic National Forest, the more I sensed disappointment rather than discovery. How could there be any surprises here for me, who had come of age in just such a place? Arriving with limited expectations, I headed almost at once for the coast.

ART WOLFE/TONY STONE IMAGES

A miles-long windrow of drift logs, debarked by the constant pounding of surf, divided Olympic's living forest from its cobbled beaches. Some trunks were sea-smoothed, others sea-splintered. All had been bleached by the sun. These were the white bones of the forest. Standing on a giant femur of Douglas fir, I looked up and down the coast—and was struck by this country's truly Olympian scale: The tall, dark headlands; the monumental sugarloafs and obelisks just offshore; the

Home both for a national park and a national forest, Washington State's Olympic Peninsula takes in up to 15 feet of rain yearly. One result: Just inland of its fractured Pacific coast (above) lies the biggest and one of the lushest temperate rain forests on earth.

giant, sea-pruned conifers; the oversized swells of the North Pacific rumbling and crashing ashore; the broad beaches all smoky with salt mist; the colossal heaps of driftwood. Barefoot, I scrambled up the windrow and began to walk the uppermost logs. Every eighth or ninth trunk, despite all its tonnage, shifted or teetered under the miniscule load of myself, forcing me to another. I had seen similar driftwood tangles at the mouths of forest rivers in the tropics, but never logs so gigantic as these. Maybe—it suddenly occurred to me—I had slighted my native forests.

Olympic National Forest contains true rain forest. The valleys of the Hoh, Queets, and Quinault Rivers, on the western side of Washington's Olympic Range, face the storms blowing in off the Pacific and receive an average of 145 inches of precipitation annually. In the odd year as many as 180 inches of rain and drizzle—15 feet—fall here.

Similarly cool and lush forests exist along the coasts of Chile, New Zealand, southern Australia, and Tasmania, but two-thirds of all such woodlands in the entire world lie right here in the Pacific Northwest. The greatest temperate rain forest on earth is our own. It begins in the red-wood country of northern California, extends along the coasts of Oregon, Washington, British Columbia, and the Alaskan panhandle, and ends in south-central Alaska. Today, much of this lush, productive ecosystem lies within our national forest system.

Of the two principal types of rain forest—temperate and tropical—tropical is much the larger. It occupies a broad, east-west band that clings fairly close to the Equator; temperate rain forest is confined to narrow coastal strips running north-south. Tropical forest is broadleaf; temperate is mostly needleleaf. Tropical is generally more ancient, having existed with little geological disturbance for millions of years—while lands of temperate rain forests are prone to repeated remodeling by glaciers. Only 14,000 years ago, for example, much of the Olympic Peninsula was under ice.

Ecologists have only begun to sort out the numerous and often complicated biological interrelationships that exist in both types of rain forest. Even so, they feel certain that tropical forests, having enjoyed hundreds of millennia of uninterrupted speciation, are more diverse. The world's temperate rain forests, they believe, produce more biomass per acre—as well as the biggest trees on earth.

The westward-facing valleys of Olympic National Forest and Olympic National Park possess what are probably the optimal conditions for temperate rain forest. Nowhere else in the world do trees grow so big so fast. To the south, the national forests of California and Oregon—Six Rivers, Klamath, and Siskiyou—are a little too dry to support such peak lushness. To the north, Alaska's Tongass and Chugach are a bit too cold. Olympic's valleys are just right.

The emblem and dominant species of the peninsula's tall, fast-growing forest is *Picea sitchensis*, Sitka spruce. We really should call it Olympic spruce, for up in Sitka a forester may need a magnifying glass to count a spruce's growth rings; on the Olympic Peninsula the naked eye is usually sufficient. The biggest known living Douglas fir, a specimen 14 feet in diameter, grows in the Queets Valley. The biggest known western hemlock, some 8 feet across, grows in the Quinault.

Western red cedar—also known locally as canoe cedar—abounds here as well. The Hoh, Quileute, and Quinault tribes once carved canoes from its aromatic, straight-grained wood, as did the Haida, Kwakiutl, and Tlingit of British Columbia and Alaska. The entire material culture of the aboriginal Pacific Northwest—canoes, lodges, implements, art, and totem poles—was hewn from cedar. Nor were Native Americans the only Pacific peoples to work native American wood. As I continued threading my way over the barkless, dead trees of my Olympian log pile, I came across the fattest trunk yet: a giant Douglas fir. It reminded me of the story of Chief Taio and his unfinished canoe.

Taio was neither Hoh nor Haida but Hawaiian. Occasionally a drift log from the Pacific Northwest caught a current to his archipelago. These errant conifers, much bigger and and more seaworthy than Hawaii's native koa trees, were appropriated by royalty and made into canoes. Two logs were required, since Hawaiian canoes are double canoes, dugouts in tandem. Drift logs from North America were few and far between on Hawaii, one of the most remote archipelagoes on earth. For years Chief Taio kept one huge, unworked Douglas fir, waiting for its twin to drift in some day from the unknown land beyond the horizon. The horizon never obliged. Finally, heartbroken, Taio had his prize log made into one of the biggest single-hulled outrigger canoes ever carved in the islands.

I wished Taio could be with me, perched on this logjam 60 yards across and miles in length. Whole fleets—armadas—of his missing log lay all about. Leaving the beach of dead and horizontal trees, I entered the forest of the living and upright. The understory was green and muted except where direct sun dappled the forest floor with incandescent hot spots. This fitful distribution of light amid reigning dimness made the understory here—much like the understory of tropical rain forest—a photographer's nightmare.

The groundcover was deer fern, oxalis, and beadruby (also known as false lily of the valley), punctuated by giant leaves of skunk cabbage—which attracts beetle pollinators in part by its stink, as do many plants of the humid tropics. The big Sitka spruces had thick, Doric trunks, well buttressed. The buttresses were not the enormous, serpentine flanges seen in tropical forests but they seemed somehow nobler. Because Sitka spruce is unable to control water loss from its needles, it prospers only in forests of high ambient wetness. This characteristic has helped make it an indicator tree for the wettest parts of the Northwest's temperate rain forest.

Here and there among the indicative spruces, I recognized trunks of western red cedar and western hemlock. As much as anything else, this quick recognition—the relatively easy identification of species—helps distinguish temperate from tropical rain forest. In tropical forest, tree diversity can be bewildering even for the tropical botanist, with hundreds of different tree species often growing on a single acre, few of those species identifiable from the trunks. But in temperate rain forest such as Olympic National Forest most trees are identifiable at a glance—the exfoliating bark of Sitka spruce, the fluted trunks of western red cedar, the connected ridges of western hemlock. This is a forest where familiarity is possible.

Olympic's trees often grow in straight lines. This linearity, another signature of temperate rain forest, stems from "nurse logs"—fallen trees—which decay much more slowly than do their counterparts in the warm tropics. Here, because they remain on the ground nearly as long as they stood in the air, they influence the next generation more directly. From moss mats blanketing such nurse logs, six-inch spruce and hemlock seedlings tend to rise in single file, aligning precisely with the log that nurtures them through its own decay. Find an older nurse log, half-rotted, and you often see big adolescent trees—a century or so old—standing in perfect colonnades. Sometimes the nurse deteriorates in such a way that spaces appear beneath the newcomer's roots, giving it a stilt-like appearance. Only under the pillars of the forest's most ancient colossi have all traces of their doting nurses vanished.

Here and there I would find a young fir or spruce or hemlock that had germinated atop the ruin of an upright snag. The young tree's roots, snaking down the host tree in search of ground, closely resembled the roots of strangler figs entwining their victims in tropical rain forest. But unlike figs, these strangler firs take root in trees that are already dead; they do not throttle their hosts alive. Thus another difference: Competition in the temperate forest is clearly robust, but seems somehow less lethal and intense than it is in tropical forests. Yet another difference concerns the shape of the forest. Here, the canopy is less continuous than in tropical rain forest, and more light reaches the forest floor. In place of the sprawling, broadleaf, "umbrella" crowns of the tropics are the conical spires of conifers. The

umbrella crown is efficient at intercepting the light of equatorial latitudes, where the sun dallies high overhead. Conical shapes are more advantageous in higher latitudes, where the sun circles lower in the sky.

TOM & PAT LEESON

Healing bark of the rare Pacific yew— a temperate rain forest species seen here in Gifford Pinchot National Forest, Washington State—contains a cancer-fighting chemical. Recent synthesis of this compound promises to benefit mankind —and to reduce the need for harvesting yews.

In tropical lowland rain forest, nutrients are quickly recycled into the wood and leaves of the plant, with very little remaining in the soil; the soil's richness is illusory. In temperate forests the soil is thick, and decaying wood lies everywhere, a great bank of nutrients. These were, at any rate, my impressions. I thought I should check them with an expert.

I found Dr. Nalini Nadkarni in the Quinault Valley at the base of a tall and mossy big-leaf maple, which she and her entomologist husband had just finished rigging with climbing rope. Dr. Nadkarni divides her time between the Olympic rain forest and the montane, tropical cloud forests of Costa Rica. She seemed the ideal person to provide an overview.

One major difference between the two forests she studies, she explained, concerns epiphytes—plants that get their moisture and nutrients directly from rainfall and dust particles in the air rather than from soil, and often grow atop other plants in order to get maximal sunlight.

"In this forest," she said, "you only get nonvascular plants as epiphytes, except for one fern." That is, the epiphytic plants that occur in Olympic consist of species that generally lack well-organized root and circulatory systems. But in the tropics, she noted, epiphytes include "a tremendous diversity of higher vascular plants as well. Orchids, bromeliads, ferns, shrubs—even trees—all growing in the canopy. No one really knows why vascular plants haven't come up with a method of making it as epiphytes in temperate rain forest. Maybe they haven't had time to evolve."

"No orchids?" I asked. Already I had seen an orchid here, one called rattlesnake plantain. It was growing on the ground, but it had looked to me like a plant that *wanted* to be up in a tree.

Dr. Nadkarni shook her head. "There are no epiphytic orchids here." She should know. Epiphytes have been her specialty ever since she was a graduate student. Trained in rock-climbing techniques in Washington State, she had brought those skills to the Hoh River Valley, applying them to the study of epiphytes high in big-leaf maples.

"I was climbing trees, taking sample swatches of epiphytes, measuring branches, then coming back and drying and weighing the epiphytes, trying to reconstruct their biomass and nutrient capital. As I cut these swatches I kept seeing root systems underneath. I thought they must be roots of the epiphytes. But then I realized, no, they can't be, because there are no vascular-plant epiphytes up there. I began tracing these root systems back, and they all ended up belonging to the host tree. It was such an amazing feeling. This is incredible! These are roots from the tree!"

Why were big-leaf maples—already well served by terrestrial roots that presumably provided them with sufficient water and nutrients—putting forth aerial root systems high up their own trunks?

"I went back to my major professor and asked him to tell me about these roots. He said 'What roots?' He had never heard of them."

Since her initial discovery, Dr. Nadkarni has found similar canopy root systems in some North American alders and cottonwoods, as well as in New Zealand's temperate rain forest and in the tropical forests of Costa Rica and Papua New Guinea. Their purpose, it seems, is to collect rent— in the form of moisture and nutrients from the arboreal "soil" that forms in the mats of epiphytes—from the tree's epiphytic tenants. Thus for all the mosses I had seen growing on Olympic's big-leaf maples, there was no free lunch. This was not the classic relationship of host and epiphyte, but true symbiosis: The trees provided supporting structure for the mosses, while the mosses provided additional moisture and food to the trees. I suggested that the old definition of epiphyte doesn't work anymore.

"That's exactly right," Dr. Nadkarni said.

Again I was struck by that very human contradiction: We make so much fuss over forests of the tropics, so little over our own. Temperate rain forests, like the tropical, are full of relationships just waiting to be discovered under the moss. In both systems certain trees put forth canopy

Snaring a sunset over Florida's Apalachicola National Forest, longleaf pines are both sun-loving and fire-resistant; after a fire, their big cones quickly open to reseed. Needles of this appropriately named species vary from 8 to 18 inches in length—while the trees range as tall as 120 feet.

JAMES RANDKLEV

roots, and symbiosis runs wild. Tropical rain forests produce natural sources of potential cancer treatments like the rosy periwinkle; temperate rain forests nurture plants with similar promise, such as the Pacific yew. In the forest canopies of Borneo, orangutans and gibbons travel miles without coming to earth; in Olympic Peninsula, arboreal weasels such as martens and fishers do the same. Flying marsupials glide through the tropical rain forest of Queensland, Australia; flying squirrels through the temperate rain forest of the Queets and the Quinault. Giant river otters swim in the Amazon's tributaries; miniature "otters"—tiny, aquatic mammals called shrew moles—swim the tributaries of the Hoh.

The Olympic forest ecosystem, for all its diversity, is just one small piece in the enormous and diverse mosaic of America's national forests. There are other types of coniferous forest throughout the West, drier but vast and equally inspiring for their particular evergreen growths. In Oregon's Siuslaw and other Pacific-slope forests, Douglas firs luxuriate amid deep, rich soils—while the foxtail pines of California's Eldorado and Stanislaus cling to clefts in obdurate granite at 11,000 feet.

Farther south, Arizona's Tonto and Coronado National Forests encompass parts of the Sonoran Desert, characterized by saguaro, cholla, prickly

Spike-flowered bromeliad flags a steamy, shadowy grove of sierra palms with a red exclamation point. The site is El Yunque, part of Puerto Rico's Caribbean National Forest— the only unit of our national forest system to contain tropical rain forest.

TONY ARRUZA

pear, and ocotillo. Then there is the "ghost forest" of Wyoming's Bridger-Teton National Forest, an expanse of blackened lodgepole snags killed by the great Yellowstone fire. Montana's Gallatin includes a forest of stone, 40 square miles of more than a hundred species of petrified trees, many of them still upright.

The nation's easternmost forests harbor a very different and even more varied mix. Some are composed of deciduous species that flame scarlet and orange and yellow every autumn. Others, such as Florida's Apalachicola, contain towering longleaf pines. Elsewhere in the same state, Osceola offers tannin-stained swamps of cypress and sweet bay and black gum, while Ocala—our only subtropical national forest—unites an overstory of longleaf pines with an understory of palmettos and wire grass. It also varies from dank wetlands to dry paleodunes.

Throughout the northern Midwest, no less than eight separate national forests celebrate our North Woods, a broad transitional zone where eastern mixed forest merges with the largely needleleaf, boreal forest of the far north. This is relatively young forest: Some portions of Minnesota's Superior National Forest lay under glacial ice a mere 10,000 years ago.

Our national forests compose a world of many extremes. There are climatic extremes: Spanning roughly 45° of latitude, national forest lands range from the truly tropical to the truly boreal. Puerto Rico's Caribbean National Forest—more commonly called El Yunque—enfolds a warm and misty zone that includes part of the nation's only tropical rain forest. Then there is our northernmost forest, Alaska's Chugach, where the advance and retreat of glaciers is an old dance, and the steps of plant succession in lower elevations are well established. First come pioneer mats of dryas—tufted, nitrogen-fixing plants that Alaskans call "Einsteins" for their wild manes—then seedlings of balsam poplar, alder, and willow. With distance from the ice front and suitable passage of time, a margin of taller balsam poplars emerges, to be replaced finally by spruce.

When it comes to extremes of height, the coast redwoods of California's Los Padres and Oregon's Siskiyou National Forests rank number one, the tallest trees on earth. At the other end of the scale are the diminutive whitebark pines of California's Inyo National Forest. Coast redwoods thrive close to sea level in a fog belt along the Pacific's edge; some whitebarks grow high in the snowbelt, near timberline, stunted by fierce winds and harsh winters. In 1963 the National Geographic Society, searching for the loftiest redwood, found one 367 feet tall. John Muir, seeking to age a particular whitebark, once counted 426 growth rings in a specimen that stood just three feet high, with a trunk 6 inches in diameter.

At one extreme of age stand the Methuselahs: the bristlecone pines, which can live for nearly 50 centuries. Close behind are the massive *Sequoiadendron giganteum*, the "big trees" of Sequoia National Forest in the Sierra Nevada. Near the other extreme are meteoric species like jack and lodgepole pines, trees never meant to grow as old but designed in their very bark and cones to flame out young.

Giant sequoias are somewhat shorter than their redwood cousins, but have far more girth. They are the most massive trees that have ever lived. One of the world's largest, the Boole Tree in the Converse Mountain region of Sequoia National Forest, stands 269 feet tall with a circumference of 112 feet and a base diameter surpassing 33 feet (opposite). John Muir once spent the better part of a day with a pocket lens atop the broadest sequoia stump he could find; he claimed to have counted more than 4,000 rings, though no one since has ever found quite so many. Muir believed the species was all but immune to disease, vulnerable only to lightning, high winds, and man once it had gotten past adolescence. "I never saw a Big Tree that had died a natural death," he wrote.

Lodgepole and jack pines, in contrast, seem made for lightning. Lodgepoles cover vast areas of the West—Shoshone, Targhee, Bridger-Teton, Custer, Deschutes, and many other national forests—growing in endless, even-age stands. Jack pines are common over many of our northern forests. Some of the cones of both species are serotinous, closed and sealed with resin. Inside each cone's clenched fist, the seeds remain viable for 25 years or more, waiting for the wildfire that will toast the cones, melt the resin, pop open the scales, and release the next generation upon the rich, black ash left by the fire. Large, killing natural fires return to these forests every 25 to 150 years—an interval which by no mean coincidence abuts the expected life span of the jack pine.

The plants within each forest are as versatile and varied as the forests themselves. Mountain hemlock and foxtail pine, for example, flourish in the coarse, shallow soils of Sierra and Inyo National Forests. Sweet bay, tupelo, and black gum, however, prefer acidic, tea-colored swamps such as occur in Osceola National Forest. At one trophic extreme are Spanish moss and orchids—ethereal plants that subsist on moisture and nutrients in the air. You can find them in South Carolina's Francis Marion National Forest, among others. Just up the coast, in North Carolina's Croatan National Forest, thrives the widest selection of carnivorous plants in the national forests: the voracious sundews, bladderworts, pitcher plants, and Venus's-flytraps. Between each set of extremes, of course, lie all gradations of forest residents and types.

The largest two-leaf piñon pine on earth, a tree with a trunk 12 feet in circumference, grows in Manti-La Sal National Forest of southeastern Utah. The world's largest Rocky Mountain juniper, the "Jardine Juniper," with a trunk 8 feet in diameter and an age of about 3,000 years, grows in Wasatch-Cache National Forest in northeastern Utah. Brewer's weeping spruce, one of the rarest conifers in the United States, grows in the snowiest hollows on the coldest north slopes of Siskiyou, Klamath, Shasta-Trinity, and Six Rivers National Forests. The wild lily called Harper's beauty grows only within the warm and humid savannas of Apalachicola in western Florida.

In my own travels from forest to forest, I found that my appreciation of this natural diversity within our national forest system steadily grew.

Homo sapiens gather round Sequoiadendron giganteum in this 1901 photo of the famed Boole Tree, Sequoia National Forest, California. The still-living colossus—largest giant sequoia in a national forest and third largest in the world—stands 269 feet tall with a 112-foot circumference.

USDA FOREST SERVICE

The experience became, in the end, almost vertiginous. I had no sooner learned to identify one set of trees and shrubs and flowers—mastered one glossary of botanical names—than I had to learn another. From amidst redwoods on a steep ridge of the Ventana Wilderness, in Los Padres National Forest, I looked down at the Pacific and its offshore beds of kelp.

It was some interface: the tallest plants of land meeting the tallest in the sea. Giant kelp are the redwoods of the macroalgae. If *Sequoia sempervirens*, the redwood, demonstrates the heights to which a vascular plant can grow, then *Macrocystis pyrifera*, the giant kelp, demonstrates the lengths to which a lowly alga can go. The stipes, or stalks, of kelp sometimes reach two hundred feet from the seafloor to the surface, where they spread their canopy of fronds. Two sea lions were swimming underwater, pale torpedo shapes gliding between the stipes. Several dozen more had hauled out, wet and black, on offshore rocks, and a few were dozing, dried to a tawny leonine color, on the rocky beach below me. The hoarse barking of the sea lions carried up the mountainside. It was not one of those animal voices one would expect in a national forest—the barking of lions—but there it was. The flotation bladders of the giant kelp rose and fell gently with the swell, and the boughs of the giant redwoods whispered in the wind.

Trumpets of pitcher plants rise up in swampier sections of South Carolina's Francis Marion National Forest, exuding a sweet nectar that lures insects down their funnel-like throats, while downward-pointing hairs bar escape. Digestive enzymes in the watery liquid at the base of each pitcher slowly disassemble the hapless victims.

TONY ARRUZA

In Kaibab National Forest, in springtime, I followed the Arizona Trail as it wandered through ponderosa pines, junipers, and sagebrush. Here and there stood Gambel oaks, bare still in late spring. The branches of these trees are sharply angular and very twiggy, each oak looking like a buzz of electricity against the calm, evergreen backdrop of ponderosa and juniper. A few ponderosas were infested with dwarf mistletoe, and every single juniper I saw was burdened by that parasite. Mistletoe infection is so universal and chronic in the Utah juniper that I began to wonder: Was it truly infection or might it be symbiosis, similar to the one Dr. Nadkarni discovered under the mosses of her big-leaf maples? I was contemplating mistletoe when suddenly the bottom dropped out of Kaibab National Forest and its Arizona Trail. The tableland of ponderosa and juniper fell away precipitously into the red and orange sandstones and schists of the mile-deep gorge of Grand Canyon. I spent an hour at the canyon rim, admiring the national park, then hiked back through the forest again.

I had forgotten mistletoe. I was contemplating, instead, the unrealized grand canyon under my feet. The words of some poet—Alexander Pope,

I believe—came to mind: "Finer forms are in the quarry than ever [Michel] Angelo evoked." Yes, and finer forms are in the sandstone than ever Colorado carved. Had a few pebbles and other surface obstacles been arranged differently, back when the river began to incise its channel, then the Colorado might have turned this way. The national park would have been here, and the national forest over there.

Tongass National Forest, the largest forest of all, is subdivided by the labyrinthine fiordland of Alaska's Inside Passage. In a kayak long ago, a friend and I traveled nearly the watery length of the Tongass, from Icy Bay to Ketchikan. Much of the outer coasts there are bluffs, sculpted by big storm waves roaring in from the Gulf of Alaska. Kayakers must pick their traveling weather carefully.

The pale granite cliffs of the Tongass, spangled at waterline by a horizon of orange starfish, are crowned with dark, contorted spruces, each tree full of character, pruned by sea winds into wild and idiosyncratic shapes. The inner shorelines of the Tongass, shielded by the forest's seaward archipelago, are often gentler terrain, and the inner, protected waters make for smoother paddling. The trees there—Sitka spruce, western red cedar, Alaska yellow cedar, western hemlock—can grow straight and huge right down to the high-tide line. The stony interior beaches are bright in the sunlight, when you visit them at midday. Enter the shoreline colonnade of trunks, though, and you enter the deepest sylvan twilight.

Paddling the straits of the Tongass, we passed sleeping seals, their pale pelts beautifully mottled with dark spots, Steller's sea lions that can weigh up to a ton each, humpback whales, minke whales, and orcas. On nearly every promontory, atop some convenient snag, perched a bald eagle looking down on us. Flocks of phalaropes parted before us, heads bobbing with each stroke of lobed feet. Pairs of murrelets looked wildly at us and dove to escape. Puffins—both tufted and horned—flew across icy tiderips ahead, as did kittiwakes.

It was then that my mind's eye recalled a very similar situation in a very different forest: Florida's Ocala National Forest. There, I saw a moorhen walk essentially on water, stepping with oversized feet across a floating mat of hyacinth, water lettuce, arrowhead, and duckweed. An immature blue heron stalked through the mat, each stride long but exceedingly slow and cautious. When I left off paddling, I could hear the rubbery sound of the heron's feet in the hyacinth. Red-bellied turtles slid off their logs as my canoe approached, while cooters plopped in. The alligators didn't budge, though; they just kept sunning themselves at water's edge.

The location was Alexander Springs, a local upwelling of the cool, artesian waters of the Florida aquifer. Cabbage palms, palmettos, and the primitive-looking cycads locally called "coontie ferns" lined the sandy shore. The scene was almost Amazonian—except when I'd spot a few streaks of autumn color in the red leaves of streamside maples and the orange-brown of turkey oaks, or sight an occasional slash pine amidst the palms. Small bass swam everywhere, and bream, and gar, and good-size mullet. From a branch above the creek, a female anhinga watched me with her yellow, snakelike eye. A male anhinga, slaty blue all over, dived for a fish, entering the water like a spear.

The bird passed like an arrow under the bow of my canoe, its dark plumage suddenly effervescent and quicksilvery with tiny bubbles. It popped up 50 feet ahead—and sparked yet another memory of another diving bird. This one was white-breasted, with blood-red eyes: a common loon. My canoe, a 17-foot Old Town this time, was drifting not the wilds of Ocala but the Boundary Waters Canoe Area Wilderness of Superior National Forest. White cedars—not cabbage palms or coontie ferns—lined the shore. Behind them stood red pines, which to me looked like little ponderosas, and the upslanted, soft-green boughs of white pines, also paper birch and balsam fir.

That night, as loons laughed their maniacal calls out on a nameless lake, I watched the stars pass through the darkened treetops, silhouetted now against the heavens. To the naked eye, their path seemed almost horizontal. In Ocala not long before, the stars had risen nearly vertically through the sparse foliage of the sand pines. The celestial mechanics brought home to me, as nothing had before, the vast reach of our national forests. These woodlands are diverse not just in their floras and faunas and seasons, but in the very march of the stars overhead. 🦐

Living symbol on a deadwood perch, a regal-eyed bald eagle surveys a vast domain in the nation's largest national forest—500-mile-long Tongass, which includes most of Southeast Alaska's coast and archipelago.

FOLLOWING PAGES: *Fading sunlight filigrees spruce and pines of a mile-high evergreen woodland in Arizona's rugged Prescott National Forest.*

KENNAN WARD; GEORGE H.H. HUEY (FOLLOWING PAGES)

Delicate tracery of rime frosts a Jeffrey pine in Inyo National Forest (above), which cloaks a 165-mile-long stretch of California's eastern High Sierra.

Before the paisleyed backdrop of a flowering manzanita, a century plant in central Arizona's Tonto National Forest serendipitously cups within its squat, spiny-leafed rosette three cones from a nearby piñon pine.

FOLLOWING PAGES: Only minutes from downtown Juneau, the massive ice towers of still-active Mendenhall Glacier overlook mist-exhaling Auke Lake—and the sprawling magnificence of Alaska's Tongass National Forest.

Drawing sustenance from the forest floor's luxuriant decay, mushrooms and dwarf bunchberries (above) make an autumnal breakthrough in Mount Hood National Forest, Oregon. Ghostly colonnade of fire-singed trunks in Siuslaw National Forest—also in Oregon—receives a morning benediction of moisture (opposite), courtesy of the Northwest coast's nurturing Pacific fogs.

FOLLOWING PAGES: *Autumn's primary colors ignite New Hampshire's White Mountain National Forest. Once nearly denuded by logging, White Mountain recovered under more enlightened management. It now remains productive timberland while luring some six million recreational visitors a year.*

CHARLES GURCHE; CARR CLIFTON/MINDEN PICTURES (FOLLOWING PAGES)

Of Forests and Trees

63

Rites of fall transfigure quaking aspens in Fishlake National Forest, named for a trout-filled, high-altitude lake amid the plateaus and mountains of central Utah.

"Only God can make a tree"—or an autumn day in Nantahala National Forest (opposite), western North Carolina. A tract of virgin woods within the forest memorializes Joyce Kilmer, author of the famous poem "Trees."

FOLLOWING PAGES: Douglas fir seedlings and blooming prairie lupine bring new life to woodlands blasted by the 1980 eruption of Mount St. Helens—now a National Volcanic Monument in Washington's Gifford Pinchot National Forest.

Siskiyou National Forest

Seeking visual poetry, the photographer's lens—here deliberately blurred—
explores the evanescent moods of mountainous Siskiyou National Forest, on the

Oregon-California border. Home of five wildernesses and five wild and scenic rivers, Siskiyou also is known as a "botanist's paradise" that contains more than 1,400 plant species, many of them rare. Its great diversity, ample solitude, and untrammeled beauty have moved some to argue that such an unusual reservoir of wild nature deserves even greater protection: national park status.

See the world in a blade of grass—or in the miniature realm of a fragile
brodiaea blossom as it opens to your gaze on a quiet forest morning (above).
Find reward and refreshment in the cool sprays of a hideaway cascade such as
Elk Creek Falls (opposite and following pages)—a perfect waystop on a trail
that takes you for a contemplative hike through an old-growth forest.

PRECEDING PAGES: Reflections and reality intermingle at the edge of Babyfoot
Lake in the serene majesty of Siskiyou's Kalmiopsis Wilderness. Striving to
balance wise resource use with the preservation of primeval wilds, the Forest
Service began setting aside specific wildernesses in 1964.

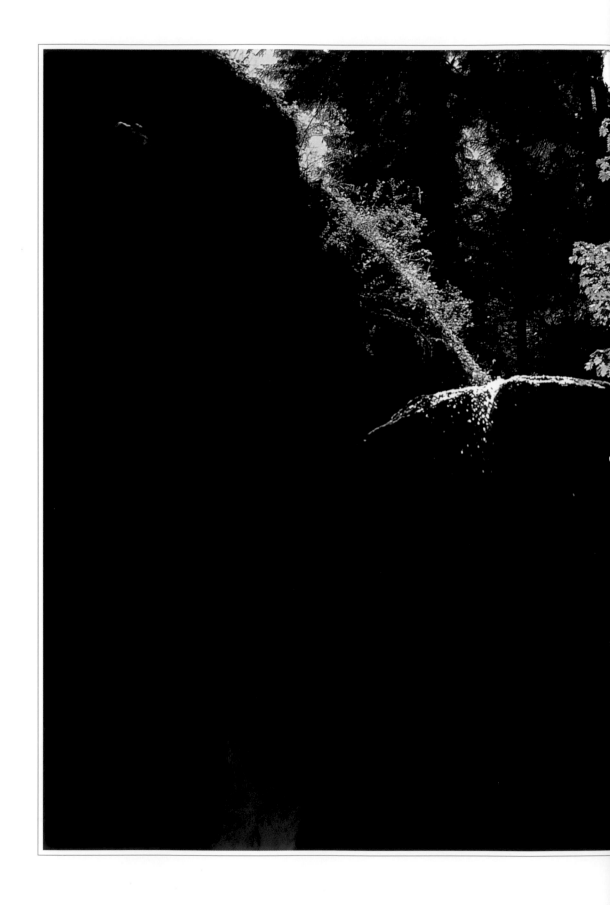

Lands of Many Uses

The civilization of aboriginal America was built of trees. In the East, the Iroquois paddled sturdy dugouts of elm and lived in longhouses covered in a clapboard of that tree's scaly, furrowed bark. The Chippewa of the North Woods framed their canoes with soft and easily splittable white cedar, then sheathed them in the bark of paper birch. Sioux, Cheyenne, Crow, and other western tribes cut poles for tepees and travois from lodgepole pine. In the Southwest, Anasazi and Mogollon cliff dwellers and their Hopi and Zuni successors built door lintels of juniper. Peoples of the Pacific Northwest hollowed seagoing canoes from canoe cedar, also called western red cedar, *Thuja plicata*. The fragrant, lightweight, straight-grained, red wood of this infinitely accommodating tree also provided the timbers for their great potlatch halls and the raw material for their totem poles, war helmets, dagger handles, bows, arrow and spear shafts, rattles, masks, storage chests, and more.

Colonial America and the young Republic that succeeded it also were built of wood. To early settlers no tree loomed as large as the white pine. Its signature use was as ship masts, so sorely needed by the Royal Navy that in time Parliament forbade the cutting of white pines by colonists. After the Revolution, these and other trees fed burgeoning cities, fleets, railroads—and various fortunes. The soft, light, close-grained wood of white pine provided nearly every kind of timber product, from walls and shingles to bobsleds and paneling. No tree in our history has been more useful—too useful for its own good, in fact, for white pine has been cut into near-oblivion, in a commercial sense. Today, noble specimens such as the 270-foot patriarch that once grew on land now occupied by Dartmouth College seem half-mythical, like trees named in some medieval herbal. Decades from now, when those second-growth and later white pines currently protected in designated wilderness areas of various national forests reach maturity, our descendants will know something of the majesty that our forefathers felled. We, for the most part, can only imagine it.

* * * * * * * * *

Movable mountain of white pine logs dwarfs lumbermen near the Ontonagon River of Michigan's Upper Peninsula, in 1893. Prized for the straight grain and easy workability of its wood, this widespread species once dominated vast areas of the Northeast and Midwest; prolonged overcutting has since all but eliminated giant individuals such as these.

Other native species also have fallen to build our nation. The yellow and slash pines of the American South provided naval stores: rosin, pitch, tar, turpentine. Ponderosa pine became the nation's foremost lumber tree as the frontier moved west, an enduring source of window sashes, doors, paneling, flooring, shelving, kitchen cabinets, moldings, jambs, and more. From the giant sugar pines of Oregon and California came bridges, barns, houses, and mine props. Redwood, wonderfully resistant to decay even when in contact with water or soil, became flumes, aqueducts, wine casks, posts, flooring, shingles, beams—and the walls of the California house in which I grew up. Farther north, in Washington and Alaska, the wonderfully tight-grained wood of Sitka spruce proved ideal for violins, pianos, racing shells, and wooden airplanes.

The grain of all these woods is ingrained in us. A sense of America's inextricable connection to its trees influenced Gifford Pinchot's declaration that the primary purpose of national forests should be to assure a steady flow of timber for homes. By the 1950s and 1960s, that flow became a flood. Our national forests produced 1.5 billion board feet of lumber in

1941, 4.4 billion in 1951, 8.3 billion in 1961, and 11.5 billion in 1970. The timber industry overcut its own lands, then turned increasingly to national forests. It grew adept at diverting the USFS from its founding principles. Traditional commitments to multiple use of forests and unevenage management of trees were often forgotten, replaced by clear-cutting and dominant use. The 1980s became an era of overcutting, both on and off Forest Service lands. Overcutting continues in many western forests today. We have come close to killing the golden goose.

Our civilization is no longer built of trees. It is built increasingly of steel and concrete, of aluminum, titanium, fiberglass, composites, and other wood substitutes. Today, 73 percent of the nation's timberland is privately owned; less than 15 percent of our lumber comes from our national forests. To most inside the Forest Service, it is apparent that the agency's mandate is changing, and the next century must bring us a new sort of national forest. The shape of that forest is still dim, its priorities still debated, but it is clear that lumber will lose primacy there.

In addition to timber, our national forests sustain a multitude of other harvests, little celebrated but sustainable. By law, these lands are managed according to the concept of "multiple use," an idea Gifford Pinchot introduced, which was later codified in the Multiple Use–Sustained Yield Act of 1960. Section One of that act reads, "It is the policy of the Congress that the national forests...shall be administered for outdoor recreation, range, timber, watershed, and wildlife and fish purposes." In 1964, wilderness preservation was added to the list of officially sanctioned activities for these "lands of many uses." Multiple-use has become the watchword for the agency, the slogan adorning its entry and exit signs, the characteristic that sets its lands apart from others.

Currently, Americans collect firewood in their national forests, also Christmas trees, sphagnum moss, deer moss, medicinal herbs, and mushrooms both magic and mundane. Southern forests produce gooseberries, summer and muscadine grapes, wild plums, persimmons. Forests from Florida through the Great Lakes out to the Pacific Northwest produce blueberries and huckleberries. In the dry washes of southwestern forests, gatherers pick jojoba beans. The hard, brown, acornlike nut of the jojoba provides useful additives to soaps, shampoos, and skin conditioners. It also can be processed into a high-quality lubricant that serves as a substitute for sperm whale oil. Perhaps the most profitable crop of the forests—the statistics, like the growers, are elusive—is marijuana. It is one harvest the Forest Service does not celebrate, and burning is the prescribed remedy.

The wood of the Southwest's piñon pines is hard, brittle, and resinous. Indians in this area used it to build pit houses, and for at least the last 15,000 years they have turned to this tree for food. Piñon nuts are lower in fat than pecans, higher in protein and carbohydrates. For the Paiutes, Apaches, Pimas, and other desert tribes, the nuts were a staple, eaten raw or in mush or in soups. Today, the piñon harvest remains a family enterprise—a harvest by the public on public lands—and the crop is worth millions of dollars annually. A Forest Service pamphlet entitled *In a Nutshell* offers one formula for harvesting:

JAMES RANDKLEV

Stark contrasts of a fresh clear-cut and standing trees collide in Washington State's Olympic National Forest. Logging—a traditional use of national forest lands— continues but is declining. Less than 15 percent of our timber needs today are supplied by USFS lands.

"Place canvas around the base of a tree," it begins. "Shake individual limbs by hand or with rakes to harvest nuts from opened cones on the tree." Unopened cones are placed in gunny sacks in the sun for several days, to dry. "Shake the sacks to free the nuts. The nuts will drop to the bottom of the sacks. The empty cones will stay on top." My kind of forestry, simple and sure.

According to Haniel Long's book, *Piñon Country*, pine nuts taste of "pine and sunshine and popcorn, and peanuts too in a way." I could taste the pine and sunshine, but was less sure of the popcorn or peanuts. While eating them I recalled the story an 80-year-old Navajo had told me years before. Chauncy Neboiya, like many Navajos of his generation, had been dragooned as a child, sent away from his family to attend a Bureau of Indian Affairs school.

"We didn't seem to get enough to eat," Chauncy had told me of his experiences at the school. "So one night we went through the window. There were three of us. This boy, Andrew, he was our leader. Andrew, Bernard Thompson, and me, we took off. We walked just almost all night. Spent a whole day living on nothin' but piñon."

So now, to me, piñon nuts taste of pine and sunshine and flight across the desert. The bright, coniferous taste links me to those three escaping Navajo boys, to the old Paiutes before them, even to Folsom Man himself. It is the very essence of the Southwest.

America's national forests harbor a wealth of other edibles as well. Hunters seasonally take white-tailed deer, mule deer, elk, bear, turkey, duck, and quail. The national forest system is a cornucopia for less glamorous game as well: raccoon, opossum, squirrel, snapping turtle. In the fast streams of western forests, fishermen hook salmon, steelhead, and their smaller cousins—cutthroat, rainbow, Apache, Dolly Varden, and other trout. The lakes and rivers of the North Woods provide lake trout, walleye, smallmouth bass, and northern pike. The waters of the southern forests teem with sunfish, catfish, buffalofish, bass, and perch.

In the peak fishing months of March through May, earthworms bring from \$25 to \$28 a can to harvesters who work the sandy soils of Apalachicola National Forest in the Florida Panhandle. In these parts, "to bait" does not mean threading worm to hook, but extracting worms from the ground. In a process known as "grunting" or "scrubbing" or "rubbing" for worms, the baiter drives a wooden stake—his stob—into the earth with hammer blows from the long bar he calls his iron. Kneeling, he grips the iron firmly at either end, palms downward. Leaning his weight into his work like a man planing wood, he strokes the length of the iron repeatedly and rhythmically over the top of the stob, producing a deep, metallic croaking. It is a call vibrant, interrogative, and alien, like the plaint of some giant frog in an iron mine on Mars.

Under Apalachicola's longleaf pines in the darkness before dawn, baiter Charles McCranie drove in a stob, then handed me his iron. My first few grunts were squeaky and pathetic. Then I bore down, surprising myself as I suddenly produced just the resonant, worm-tingling grunt I was after. I hit the stob three or four good licks—and pale legions of annelids magically began to emerge from their tunnels. I had become a pied piper of worms. The finest bait in the entire South—the finest, some say, in the whole of the planet—was surfacing all around me.

Far beneath the earthworms, below even the root systems of many forests, lie lodes of gold, silver, turquoise, copper, coal, oil, and other mineral resources. Since the very beginning of national forests, mining has been an approved use on these lands. It has yielded astounding mineral riches and has opened a Pandora's box of abuses.

In Pueblo Canyon of Tonto National Forest's Sierra Ancha Wilderness, for example, you can still see the dark entrance to an exploratory mine punched in the rock, near some ancient cliff dwellings. Once thought to contain commercial quantities of uranium, Sierra Ancha drew swarms of prospectors in the 1950s. Very little radioactive rock was extracted from Sierra Ancha, but prospector's diggings and roads remain even now, still eroding the land.

MICHAEL H. FRANCIS

Sighting in on sport, a bow hunter in camouflage and face paint takes aim amid the aspens of Montana's Gallatin National Forest. Americans spend some 16 million user-days a year hunting on national forest lands. Their prey ranges from big game to squirrels to migratory birds.

They point up snags in the theory of multiple use—what possible alternative uses can there be for mine tailings or for slash-strewn clear-cuts? They also underline the problematic nature of mining our national forests.

The Mineral Land Act of 1866 and the Mining Law of 1872 gave miners wide-open access to public lands, in order to speed settlement and development of the then-wild West. Still on the books, these old laws have for decades hamstrung the Forest Service and other agencies charged with administering public lands. Mining has proved itself a voracious consumer of public trees, lawfully (but often wastefully) using the timber on claims for bridges, railroad ties, flumes, mine props, and as fuel for locomotives or the steam boilers of crushing mills. Whole forests of the Sierra Nevada disappeared into the shafts of the Comstock Lode. Longwall mining of coal in Utah's Manti–La Sal National Forest caused the forest above to subside by several feet. In addition to major mining sites, countless small claims—many of them dubious—have come to dot our national forests. Some "miners" have really been loggers, dedicated more to cutting timber on their claims than to extracting any mineral resources there. Others seem more interested in the land's recreational appeal. Take Angeles National Forest, not far from Los Angeles. It is mineral-poor compared to other California national forests, yet its proximity to the city has made it one of the state's leading mining-claim forests. Just satisfy the minimal legal requirements for a claim and you can put up all the cabins you want there.

For years the Forest Service has had tools to remedy some abuses. The Surface Mining Reclamation Act of 1977, for example, requires that mined national forest lands be restored to a condition allowing renewed multiple use. But harmonizing mineral exploitation with other uses remains unfinished business in our national forests.

"If there is magic on this planet, it is contained in water," wrote the poet and naturalist Loren Eiseley. I remembered his words in the desert of Tonto National Forest, as my son and I watched Horton Springs emerge, sudden and full-throated, from the base of a sun-parched wall of the Mogollon Rim. The water cascaded through green and mossy talus, then dropped through a riparian zone of horsetails and broad-leafed aquatic plants before leveling out into interconnected pools of watercress.

"If you were a man, you'd wade in," my ten-year-old dared me. I did. The water was achingly cold after Tonto's heat, but I was able to smile back a challenge to David. He stepped in, screamed, and leaped back to the bank. Brook trout were everywhere, shooting off to take refuge in deeper pools or under farther mats of watercress. We nibbled the cress, its leaves as peppery hot as the water was cold. Maples, walnut trees, alder, even big Douglas firs shaded us in this desert oasis; various animal tracks pocked the shore. It was the old miracle of water in the desert, and it seemed to me that Eiseley was right.

Many in the Forest Service believe that water is the most important treasure of our national forests. Uncompromised watersheds provide clean water and consistent streamflow for fish and wildlife—as well as for downstream municipalities and irrigators. When logging, grazing, and road-building are well managed throughout a given watershed, that land retains its capacity to mitigate floods and recharge groundwater aquifers. Watershed protection is particularly important in the arid West, where water issues promise to dominate political and environmental debates in the future as they have in the past.

East of the Sierra Nevada on a narrow blacktop road through the sagebrush hills of Toiyabe National Forest, I slowed for a herd of cattle that preceded two dusty cowboys in chaps and flat-brimmed Stetsons. As men and animals disappeared into the cloud of their own dust and the pungence of sage, I found myself contemplating how much of our national

RAYMOND GEHMAN

Success comes to ten-year-old Andy Gehman in the form of a northern pike at Ottertrack Lake, part of Superior National Forest's Boundary Waters Canoe Area Wilderness. Anglers account for an estimated 37 million user-days within the national forest system every year.

forests are sagebrush deserts. *If this is a forest then where are the trees?*

I remembered something that Andrew Colaninno, district ranger in Florida's Apalachicola National Forest, once told me concerning Apalachicola's forest of wire grass and longleaf pine. "There's an unusual way of thinking about these forests that I've adopted," he said, "because I think it's ecologically right. What we're dealing with here is not a forest that happens to have grass in the understory; what we're dealing with is a shortgrass prairie that just happens to have trees on it."

Similarly, much of the West is sagebrush desert that just happens to have junipers, or palo verde, or mesquite on it. Or saguaros, or piñons, or ponderosas. No such country of incidental trees produces millions of board feet of lumber, and the principal economic use for these lands of little rain has always been as rangeland.

Amid the rolling, dry-grass range of Arizona's Tonto National Forest—which just happens to have scattered junipers on it—Alberto Holquin stood beside his water truck, looking to the southeast. It was early morning, and each squat, rounded juniper cast a thin but long shadow hundreds of feet westward. Holquin (page 88) was 68 years old, dark-haired and fit, a native of Chihuahua who now lived in Chandler, Arizona. His face was full of the strength of the Mexican paisano, brown and seamed and humorous, punctuated by startlingly blue eyes. His ancient water truck had a post-apocalyptic look, patched and cannibalized and jumbled with gear. Old but lively, it bumped along the uneven grassland spouting water sporadically, like a whale. Now it was parked, the cab door open, revealing a plastic cooler and satchel on the seat.

Beyond stretched the Heber-Reno Sheep Driveway, a two-mile-wide "highway" along which sheepherders—Basques, predominantly—have for most of this century trailed sheep from winter range in the Salt River Valley to summer range in the Apache-Sitgreaves National Forest. For 36 years, Holquin and his truck have met the sheep at dry stretches along this route. The current drive, Alberto intimated, could be the last.

"Too many problems," he told me. In halting English sprinkled with Spanish he explained that there were many more fences now—the old complaint of western cattlemen and sheepmen. There also was the present drought, the worst in 80 years. Never before in Alberto's 36-year career had drought forced him to truck water to this particular spot. For decades, in fact, the river of sheep itself has been drying up, dropping from 40 flocks in 1960 to only two today—about 2,000 head each. "This year, no more men from Espagne," he added. No more Basque shepherds. In their place were Chileans, working on three-year contracts. They were good men, Alberto hastened to add. They could shoe a horse quickly and were good with rope. All the same, it was sad.

Gradually the white vanguard of one flock appeared among distant junipers, the sheep welling out of the trees and flowing upslope toward us. Two Chileans trailed at the rear, one on a pinto pony, the other on foot, holding a shepherd's staff. A pair of border collies worked the flanks, turning and reintegrating the flock whenever it metastasized into separate bunches. Smoothly the approaching sea of fleece parted to flow around the water truck. As sheep milled about, the dogs drank from a bowl set out by one of the shepherds. Then Alberto hooked up a hose and with a clear, sluicing arc commenced filling some dusty troughs. Sheep rushed forward, mobbing the instant, artificial waterhole. Now and again a thirsty animal at the rear would slam-dance forward over the backs of those in its way. None of the undersheep seemed to mind the scrabbling hooves and bad manners of those above. One Chilean washed his hands in the stream from the hose, then bent to drink. I flinched; the Forest Service warns visitors to Tonto to treat all drinking water. Alberto had filled his tank at Haigler Creek, along which recreational camping is heavy. This shepherd seemed to hail from a time before giardiasis.

But then everything here seemed to belong to another era. The Chileans still used shepherd's crooks, tools that were old even when Moses was young. Their burro carried wooden water barrels as tight and well crafted as wine casks—not the lighter, ubiquitous plastic containers of today. I watched one shepherd walk the edge of the flock, wolf-eyed, surveying for lameness or other weaknesses. Suddenly his curved crook darted in, deftly hooking the foot of a black sheep. A big syringe appeared from his pocket; he injected antibiotic into the animal, then let it scramble to its feet and rejoin the flock. Again his staff darted, this time snagging a white animal. The shepherd speedily hog-tied it and carried it to the water truck. "Gorda," Alberto noted approvingly. A fat one. At the moment, this flock numbered exactly 1,925 sheep; tonight there would be 1,924.

Transhumance, the seasonal movement of livestock between different elevations and pastures, is a practice as old as animal husbandry. It mimics the seasonal migrations of wild ungulates, and since time immemorial it has enabled pastoral peoples to carve a livelihood from landscapes of low productivity. If livestock populations are kept within the capacity of their ranges, transhumance is a sensible and sustainable way of converting poor land into meat, milk, wool, and other products. But if the numbers rise too high, transhumance can be ruinous, as the spreading desertification of North Africa dramatically attests. The Wild West witnessed extreme overstocking of some rangelands, and in 1906 the Forest Service responded with a program of grazing management. The range-livestock industry, however, often resisted both the regulation and enforcement of more comprehensive management plans—largely by dominating the politics and economics of the West. The result was a legacy of degraded range. Damage has been particularly worrisome in riparian areas, for streamside ecosystems are critical to clean water, flood control, fish and wildlife habitat, and other aspects of a healthy watershed. Of course, it is precisely these areas that draw domestic livestock.

For the damage sheep caused the high meadows of his beloved Sierra Nevada, John Muir called them "hooved locusts." The bad reputation sheep have in the West stems partly from slander by cattlemen, partly from Anglo-American resentment of the Mexicans, Basques, and others who

Providing when nature fails, Alberto Holquin (right) trucks water to dry stretches along established sheep trails within two Arizonan national forests, Apache-Sitgreaves and Tonto (opposite). Grazing of private livestock on public lands has been a fact of life for generations; currently, nearly 100 million acres of our national forest system are allotted to this use.

RAYMOND GEHMAN

drive the flocks. Still, much of it was earned by the sheep themselves. At the moment, sheep are a diminishing problem on public range; declining markets for lamb and wool—not higher grazing fees or stiffer regulations from the Forest Service—have brought their numbers down dramatically. It has been hard on sheepmen but good for the range.

One evening as the grassland turned red-gold in the low-angle light, each rounded juniper now cast a long, thin shadow to the east. The Chileans' pony and pack-burro, both hobbled, grazed slowly through the short grass. Uphill under a big alligator juniper, Alberto Holquin had set his folding cot. A nearby oak sheltered the cots and canvas bedrolls of the shepherds, as well as one collie, already asleep. A sheepskin saddle blanket aired on a low branch; several newly washed shirts dried on a line strung higher up. The flock roamed a nearby hollow, audible thanks to a few belled ewes. One of the Chileans prepared the evening meal, cutting up the last of some lamb left from lunch and tossing it into a pot. Turning on a boom box, he found a Spanish-language station; the notes of a Mexican ballad blended with the smoke of his fire. Judiciously he sprinkled some spices on the lamb,

delicately sniffing the result. Then he seized the salt and upended it, sending a white avalanche into the pot—as if he had abruptly given up cooking the meat and had decided instead to preserve it. The sizzling lamb smelled wonderful despite its saltiness, the juniper smoke fragrant and evocative of an older West.

FOLLOWING PAGES: Gathering thunderstorm crowns Colorado's Comanche National Grasslands, one of 20 such units in the national forest system. Once ravaged by Dust Bowl drought, Comanche now supports deer, pronghorn, swift foxes, doves, quail, and lesser prairie chickens.

The other Chilean sat on his cot with a well-worn rifle, feeding in a couple of rounds. Alberto talked of a bear he had seen in this very spot last year. "Maybe he comes back tonight," he said with a laugh. He recalled another drive, on which a mother bear with a trio of cubs had killed five sheep, then told us of a friend who had lost 50 sheep to a single mountain lion. The lion had eaten nothing. The bear, on the other hand, had either eaten or cached all it killed. Alberto began another story. The setting sun reddened the juniper tops. The day's stunning heat was memory. The air was warm and sensual, flavored with dry grass and juniper, quiet except for the muted clangor of sheep bells. Another day's work was done.

*Mossy with disuse, an abandoned cattle chute in Montana's
Lolo National Forest (above) recalls busier times, when
grazing the public trust was considered a birthright.*

*Wild and white stretch of Tanner Creek (opposite) in Mount
Hood National Forest, Oregon, symbolizes the importance
of watershed protection, a traditional goal for forest lands.*

*FOLLOWING PAGES: "Lonely tenant of the loneliest spot on
earth," Mark Twain called California's Mono Lake, more
recently famed for its towers of calcium-rich tufa. It is
part of Inyo National Forest, primary watershed for Los
Angeles; decades of excessive water withdrawals for the city
reduced Mono to a shrunken desert basin that has only
recently begun to recover.*

Gash of an open-pit gold mine called West Generator gouges the land in Nevada's Humboldt National Forest, most heavily mined unit of the national forest network. Some 9,000 "mining occurrences"—ranging from single oil

RAYMOND GEHMAN

derricks to gigantic excavations visible from space—pattern our federal forests today. Current laws governing the mining of public lands and the setting of government royalties date back more than a century.

Getting prime sawlogs for pulp prices, Ketchikan Pulp Company pays the Forest Service only a few dollars, on average, for each tree it cuts in Tongass National Forest—while the USFS deducts the price of building logging roads.

FOLLOWING PAGES: *Alternating bands of standing trees and clear-cuts pattern the fragmented ecosystem of Oregon's Mount Hood National Forest (foreground), while distant Mount Jefferson towers over nearby Willamette National Forest.*

Ocala National Forest

As basic to a forest as trees, a forest's watershed provides the circulation vital to the ecosystem. A shining example is Florida's Ocala National Forest, where

spring-fed waters fill three main rivers amid numerous pine forests, sustain
large numbers of plant and animal species, and provide unlimited opportunities
for human recreation: swimming, hiking, camping, fishing, hunting, and
observing nature. This little blue heron takes flight from Alexander Springs, one
of four wilderness areas in this oldest national forest east of the Mississippi.

Twisted trunks of scrub live oaks (above) compete for light, water, and nutrients with the longleaf pines and wire grasses that naturally dominate many areas of Ocala's sandy, impoverished soil.

Fringed by lush growths of ferns and other water-loving plants, Fern Hammock (opposite) is part of the Lake George watershed, which supports large numbers of fish, waterfowl, and other creatures, especially in winter. Anglers, swimmers, boaters, and nature lovers also flock here in all seasons.

FOLLOWING PAGES: Far from its African home, a blue tilapia fins through Ocala's Silver Glen Springs. This algae-eating exotic species was first brought here to test its feasibility as sport fish, and somehow it escaped. Its tendency to compete for spawning grounds makes it unwelcome to native bluegill, but local largemouth bass have developed a taste for tilapia.

Wilderness and Wildlife

Mogollon Baldy, in New Mexico's Gila Wilderness, rises to an elevation of 10,770 feet; the mountain's lookout tower rises 40 feet more. My son David and I, hiking up from our camp at Snow Park, paused occasionally to study the spoor of the mountain lion that had preceded us up the trail. The lion was smallish, a female probably. She had come this way a day or two before. Now and again one of us halted to inscribe, with toe of boot, a circle around a large and perfect hoofprint. The lioness had been preceded up this trail by a bull elk.

We entered an aspen grove. The bright, quaking, spring-green canopy closed over us, and the white trunks grew thickly all around. The trunks were graduated at irregular intervals with black, inverted chevrons—the scars left when the aspens, in racing one another up toward the light, had shed their lower branches. Here and there the whiteness of the bark was marred by the dark calligraphy of old accidents. The smooth white pillar of an aspen repairs itself, after injury, with black, raised keloids and cicatrices, making it irresistible to humans with pocketknives, and irresistible also to lions. Just off the trail, my son found an aspen on which a big lion, surrendering to artistic impulse, had flexed its back and sharpened its claws high on the trunk.

On reaching the summit, we stopped to study the tight little cabin where the fire lookouts of Mogollon Baldy pass the fire season. A collecting pipe ran from the catchment of the roof down to an underground reservoir protected by a pile of stones. The water level figured to be low in the present drought. It would rise with the monsoon of late summer, provided the rains did not fail again. A pair of boots was airing on the porch, tongues lolling. We walked over to the foot of the tower. Through the lookout's open door, high above, I could see the blue-jeaned leg of one of the two women who manned the place, propped languorously on the back of a chair.

I was looking forward to meeting them. One, I had been told, had spent 13 fire seasons in this tower; her companion had been coming nearly as

long. I was full of questions. These ascetic women, in their high mountain perch surrounded by wilderness, were following a path I had once contemplated myself.

It was my late teens when I had first imagined that working in a lookout tower or lighthouse would be the perfect job. I would have to check the horizon now and then for smoke, of course, but there would be plenty of time for self-improvement. Plenty of solitude and no distractions. I would learn French and Spanish fluently, master the guitar, lift weights, and become a writer, finally knocking out all the stories that I had vaguely plotted but never set down.

Now in middle age and a little wiser, I doubted I would have accomplished quite so much. Still, this sort of wilderness exile had deep appeal.

View from Mogollon Baldy: Amid springtime's green rush of aspens and ponderosa pines, enduring scorch marks bear witness to a wildfire's spotty passage through part of America's first wilderness area—the Gila, in New Mexico's Gila National Forest.

The rewards would be great, I guessed, but so would the privations. How did the two women handle the boredom? At first, the 360° vista from the fire tower—Mogollon Range, Diablo Range, Tularosa Range, Black Range, the whole of the Gila Wilderness along with most of the rest of Gila National Forest—must have seemed as wide as all the world. But after the fifth or sixth year wouldn't that horizon begin to tighten, like a noose?

My son was ready to climb the tower's metal stairs. I hesitated. The hike had begun as a kind of pilgrimage, but I was uneasy now. Was it good manners to invade the privacy of these women? A Forest Service sign at the foot of the stairs requested visitors not to climb.

"Does the sign really mean it?" I shouted up. The stiff breeze blowing over the dome of Mogollon Baldy blew my question away. "Can we come up?" I bellowed, louder. The languorous leg came down off the chair. The leg's owner walked out on the deck and looked down from the rail, revealing brown eyes above a lush, Mexican-bandit-style moustache. Then a companion appeared, wearing dark, wraparound shades, a straw cowboy hat, and a heavy, black, five-day stubble of beard.

"Come on up," Moustache said.

By the time we reached the top of the three flights of stairs, they had swept out and neatened up for us. Moustache—Johnny Zapata—was still gripping the broom. He and Gilbert Jimenez, we learned, had been on duty only two weeks, in relief of the two female regulars.

"The girls are coming back this afternoon," Zapata said happily, adding that both he and Jimenez were desperate for relief. They were going crazy, he said, gesturing with his broom at the surrounding wilds.

Big windows gazed at the encircling mountains. The Southwestern air, normally the nation's clearest, was hazy today. A huge fire in Arizona's Tonto National Forest had just been contained; smaller blazes were still burning here in New Mexico. This was to be a spring of smoke. In one corner of the room stood a woodstove with a washbasin on top and firewood stacked neatly beneath. In another corner, a plank desk held a walkie-talkie and a pair of binoculars. On a high shelf sat the skull of a mountain lion. Its jaw was dislocated, the lower fangs thrust forward. The big underbite gave the skull a dull-witted and prognathous look, an expression such as no cougar ever displayed in life. The lion's empty orbits gazed down the west slope of the Mogollons past dark, descending ridges of spruce, Douglas fir, and aspen toward the distant, superheated plain of Cactus Flat and Little Dry Creek. The lookout floor was of blond hardwood, polished to a dull shine by the feet of fire sentinels as they shuffled about their duties. At the room's center was what appeared to be some sort of combination sundial-gunsight. The dial held a circular map of the Gila Wilderness, across which lay a reference bar ending in the gunsight. "That's our fire-finder," Zapata said. "We get an azimuth with that."

Eternally off-limits to the sawyer, this conky old snag in Gila Wilderness Area provides ready perches for raptors, as well as prime habitat for cavity-nesting birds and other wildlife. Eventually its nutrients will return to the soil for recycling.

RAYMOND GEHMAN

Johnny Zapata has worked for the Forest Service since 1978, Gilbert Jimenez since 1986. The Mexican border lies just south of Gila National Forest, and the inflections of the old country are strong in the accents of both men. Their normal jobs are in range management. Early in his career, Zapata did some time in fire towers, but never in a spot so isolated. At least there had been roads to those towers; this mountaintop was disconnected from the world. "You read everything you get your hands on," he said. "We've been reading the backs of coffee cans. We told each other all the stories we know, Gilbert and me. And that was in the first 15 minutes."

As we talked, Zapata took occasional, absent-minded swipes at the floor with his broom, just for something to do. There was no pattern to his sweeping and no need for it, as the floors were perfectly clean. We all shook our heads over the indomitability of the two women, who obviously possessed internal resources that we all lacked. For Jimenez and Zapata,

13 days in the wilderness tower had been more than enough. One of the women had spent 13 *years* here. Jesus himself left the wilderness after 40 days; these women kept coming back.

We never did meet the women; I wished I could have asked them what life was like here. My own career, I contemplated, has seen me flit around the globe from place to place, giving me an understanding of the planet that is both remarkably broad and extraordinarily shallow. What would it be like to immerse oneself in a single landscape for 13 years?

From the foot of the fire tower we looked back up toward our hosts, standing mournfully at the rail. Zapata, still holding the broom, gave us a disconsolate little wave good-bye.

As we left the bald summit to enter a grove of altitude-gnarled spruces, I paused to scan the entire horizon one last time. Geronimo and his men had known this circle well, scanning it not for wisps of smoke but for dust of cavalry. The Apaches were nomads, always moving. Geronimo could not have known this particular circle as the two women now do, for they have had to traverse the horizon every ten or twenty minutes with binoculars. Each dip and prominence has been imprinted, surely, on their memories: Whitewater Baldy, Center Baldy, Seventy-four Mountain, Bearwallow Mountain, Skeleton Ridge, Granite Peak; a continuous, undulant line where mountains meet sky. As very old women, I bet myself, these two will still retain the image of this circle; the same rolling line before me now will be the last thing to fade in their memories.

The fire tower on Mogollon Baldy looks out upon not just a circle of unspoiled mountains but at the contours of an idea. Gila Wilderness was the first designated wilderness in the United States. The idea that it incarnates—wilderness preservation—is very new. At the beginning of the 19th century, the notion that the Gila or any other wild landscape might be worth preserving would have struck any European-American as outlandish. A medieval conception of wilderness still held sway. The Anglo-Saxon *wylder ness* translates to "lair of a wild beast." It means forests, the havens of witches and satanic beings that bewitched and bewildered any human trespassers. Wilderness was a thing to cut back; to defeat. Then came Emerson and Thoreau, and Muir.

By the end of the 19th century the notion that untrammeled nature had its own allure and value had been firmly established in the public consciousness. With Muir's death in 1914, the torch passed to a Mid-westerner named Aldo Leopold.

Leopold worked 19 years for the Forest Service. He was an avid hunter and a dedicated ecologist. He also was a gifted and powerful writer, like Emerson, Thoreau, and Muir before him. "Man always kills the thing he loves, and so we the pioneers have killed our wilderness," Leopold wrote. "Some say we had to. Be that as it may, I am glad I shall never be young

Apostle of change, forester Aldo Leopold arrived in the Southwest in 1909 and soon realized that the native wildlife was disappearing. He became a lifelong advocate of wilderness, and nudged the USFS toward a policy of multiple use of natural resources.

COLLECTION OF THE UNIVERSITY OF WISCONSIN—MADISON ARCHIVES

without wild country to be young in. Of what avail are forty freedoms without a blank spot on the map?"

Like Thoreau and Muir, Leopold was not content to leave his ideas on paper. He worked tirelessly to give actual boundaries to that blank spot on the map. He fell in love with the Southwest, and one day began to ruminate on how few wild areas remained in his district. Was there some way to preserve the Gila canyon country and all it contained—the forests of ponderosa pine, fir, and aspen, the Rocky Mountain mule deer and the beautiful Sonoran white-tailed deer, the pronghorn and the black bears, the javelinas and wild turkeys, the rare and colorful Gila trout?

In 1921 he began advocating that portions of Gila National Forest be designated as a wilderness area or national hunting ground. He conceded that most foresters—particularly those steeped in Pinchot's utilitarian, commodity-centered ideology—were unhappy with the wilderness idea, but he was confident that "they will come around later." His prediction has been largely correct. On June 3, 1924, some 750,000 acres of Gila were set aside as wilderness, closed to all works of man, accessible only by foot or on horseback. Over the next 40 years the Forest Service would declare another 8 million acres of wilderness across the nation, on its administrative authority alone. With the passage of the Wilderness Act in 1964, such designations were made law.

"In wilderness you can kind of get in contact with the reality of your whole past," John Kramer told me. He is the Forest Service ranger who oversees wilderness trails and all outfitters and guides in the Wilderness Ranger District, which includes 80 percent of the Gila Wilderness. "Man is, after all, a mammal, an animal," he went on. "I think when you live in total civilization, you kind of lose track of that. You lose track of where we're going, and what our goals and our objectives are. Wilderness is a great place to get that straightened out."

Wilderness is "where the hand of man has not set foot," according to the playful definition of David Brower. Not my son, but his grandfather by the same name. Wilderness is where my father's environmentalism began. His career has been a gradual metamorphosis from young rock climber in the Sierra Nevada into what he is today, an 84-year-old activist preoccupied with the whole biosphere. In his origins he is not alone, he likes to point out. Wilderness is where we all started.

"Your gene code remembers, in important ways, the day life began on earth," he writes in *The Life and Times of David Brower*. "Everyone now living is directly connected with that day, some three and a half billion years ago....The baton of life was passed on perfectly in the ultimate relay race through time. It, not books, built your intuition, letting you know at a glance where this nettle, danger, lies between you and this flower, safety. And here you are, three and a half billion years old and hardly showing your age.

"Why? Because your beginnings were honed in the pulling and tugging, the trial and error, the success and failure, the symbiotic relationships, the teamwork, the need for life if you will, in wilderness. Civilization is too new to have interfered with your becoming."

"In wildness is the preservation of the world," Thoreau wrote.

In *This Is the American Earth*, writer Nancy Newhall observes, "The wilderness holds answers to more questions than we yet know how to ask."

Wilderness areas are sparse in forests of the East, for the wilderness idea arrived too late there. Indeed, it was the destruction of such wild lands that inspired the wilderness idea. In White Mountain National Forest of New Hampshire and Maine, there is the Presidential Range–Dry River Wilderness, protecting wild routes to the summit of Mount Washington. Vermont's Green Mountain National Forest boasts Lye Brook and Bristol Cliffs Wildernesses. In West Virginia's Monongahela National Forest there are five wildernesses, among them Otter Creek Wilderness, with its insectivorous sundews, its rhododendrons and mountain laurel.

The North Woods has wilderness areas as well—Rainbow Lake Wilderness, with its cross-country skiing trails; Whisker Lake Wilderness, where the fishing is superb; Boundary Waters Canoe Area Wilderness of Minnesota's Superior National Forest, where the canoeing is indeed superior. The South also has wild preserves, such as Louisiana's Kisatchie Hills Wilderness, Arkansas's Caney Creek Wilderness, and Florida's Juniper Prairie Wilderness. But it is in the national forests of the West that the vast majority of our designated wildernesses reside.

The northern Rockies hold the largest concentration of Forest Service wilderness lands—some ten million acres—more than any other region in the nation. Montana's Anaconda-Pintler Wilderness is a land of rugged peaks and alpine lakes. Also in Montana, the Bob Marshall Wilderness sets aside a slice of the Paleozoic Era complete with fossil trilobites; Great Bear Wilderness preserves a remnant chill of the Pleistocene in its surviving glaciers. Lewis and Clark National Forest contains the eastern section of the Bob Marshall Wilderness and its Chinese Wall, a limestone escarpment 15 miles long and 1,000 feet high. In Custer National Forest there is the Absaroka-Beartooth Wilderness and its wonderful Grasshopper Glacier, a mile-long river of ice entombing millions of grasshoppers that swarmed over the Beartooth Mountains two centuries ago. Dense forests mark the Spanish Peaks Wilderness of Montana's Gallatin National Forest, while Wyoming's Bridger Wilderness has 20 peaks higher than 12,000 feet. Grizzlies still roam Kootenai's Cabinet Mountains Wilderness in northern Montana, and bison graze the North Absaroka Wilderness of Wyoming's Shoshone National Forest.

There are scores of other wildernesses, each with its special habitats and creatures, ranging from alpine tundra through all types of forest to rivers and lakes that are home to various fish and animals, some of them rare. Each of these wilder areas of our national forests are a *wylder ness* indeed, a lair of wild beasts. But so too, are the rest of our national forest lands. Many of the nation's threatened and endangered species find their last refuge in national forests. Mount Pinos, in Los Padres National Forest, is the only home on earth for the Mount Pinos chipmunk and the Mount Pinos blue grouse. The Navajo race of the Abert squirrel, distinguished by large, tufted, pointy, squirrel-from-the-Planet-Vulcan ears, lives only in Manti–La Sal National Forest of Utah. Coronado National Forest, in southern Arizona, is home to a wild cat (the jaguar), a very rare bird (the elegant trogon), and a rare fish (the Gila topminnow). One of America's most endangered fish, the unarmored threespine stickleback, occurs in a couple of streams in Angeles National Forest, California. Arizona's Tonto National Forest protects ten species of threatened or endangered fish. The last forty Puerto Rican parrots in the wild dwell in Caribbean National Forest. Spotted owls and marbled murrelets—two poster animals of the moment for endangered residents of old-growth forest—nest in the big conifers of Siskiyou National Forest in Oregon. Gifford Pinchot's pronouncement that national forests need not be preserved as the homes of wild creatures that live there not only bucks popular sentiment today but also runs contrary to current law.

Recently I sat in the office of Andrew Colaninno, a district ranger of Florida's Apalachicola National Forest. Colaninno had just announced measures to protect a local species, *Diplocardia mississippiensis*, in its underground lairs. Outside his window, a group of angry grunters—as the hunters of *D. mississippiensis* call themselves—were demonstrating.

"Our basic founding legislation is the National Forests Management Act of 1976," Colaninno explained to me. "There is a requirement in the NFMA regulations that we maintain a viable population of all native species of animals on national forest land. In some ways, it's more restrictive than the Endangered Species Act. Under the Endangered Species Act, extirpation of a species from here would be permissible if there were loads of that same animal 20 miles away. Under NFMA, if a species is indigenous here, we have to maintain a viable population here."

The implications of NFMA, he pointed out, extend not only to big, spectacular species or to adorable ones, but to everything that runs or flies or swims or crawls. *Diplocardia mississippiensis* is an earthworm. On first coming to Apalachicola, Colaninno observed heavy commercial exploitation of the worm despite a lack of information on its abundance, its life history, or its rate of reproduction. By allowing unlimited harvests of worms, he worried, the Forest Service might be violating NFMA.

A forester with a degree in silviculture, Colaninno at first knew nothing of earthworms. He went to the University of Georgia for a crash course on the subject, and even now makes annual pilgrimages to confer with worm researchers and catch up on the latest. To some, his preoccupation with worms might seem laughable. But as Charles Darwin pointed out, earthworms are essential components of their ecosystems. Much of the life in Apalachicola National Forest, including red-cockaded woodpeckers and other endangered species, depends on calcium cycling by earthworms. That's why Colaninno raised the permit fee and imposed restric-tions on the size of the worm catch. He earned the enmity of grunters but also gratitude, let us hope, in the collective unconscious of multitudes of worms.

In some areas, Forest Service biologists have tried to reintroduce animals that have vanished. The wolf is an example. About 50 years ago, just as the federal government

JEFF GNASS

Sawtooth jags crown John Muir Wilderness area in Sierra National Forest. Naturalist, wilderness rambler, champion of the national park movement and founder of the Sierra Club, Muir believed, "The clearest way into the Universe is through a forest wilderness."

finally succeeded in its long campaign to eradicate wolves from the West, Aldo Leopold began advocating the return of wolves to a few wild areas in the Rockies. On January 14, 1995, long after his death, that dream became reality. Four Canadian wolves were brought in crates to Idaho's Salmon and Challis National Forests. A delegation from the Lemhi Tribe of Shoshones said a prayer over these pioneers, then the crates were transported to the banks of the Salmon, in the Frank Church River of No Return Wilderness. A black, 90-pound male, named "Moonstar Shadow" by Idaho's elementary school students, was first. Gently prodded out of his cage by biologists, he trotted through a grove of ponderosa pines and disappeared downriver. Another male and two females followed, scattering in different directions. It was an emotional moment; the four lines of wolf tracks were eloquent there on the shore of the Salmon. They marked a giant step for wolfkind, and for humankind as well.

That same year, radio-collared Texas cougars were released in Pinhook Swamp of Osceola National Forest. They were stand-ins for a slightly different subspecies—the all but extinct Florida panther. The cougar, *Felis concolor*, has the widest distribution of any cat on earth, from the tip of Tierra del Fuego to high in the Canadian steppes. Its Florida subspecies, *Felis concolor coryi*, once ranged from eastern Texas to the Carolinas and south to the Everglades. Today, that range has been reduced to almost nothing; only 50 or so cats remain, all in Florida's extreme southwest. Isolated from other subspecies of cougars, they have no recourse but to inbreed, and genetic problems are already apparent. Biologists feel that Texas cougars, their closest relatives, have the best chances of successfully testing the waters of Pinhook Swamp.

The bighorn sheep, John Muir believed, would be safe always in its remote homeland of the western mountains. One of his favorite animals, it preferred the same habitat Muir did—the high granite of the Sierra Nevada. Wrote Muir, "Possessed of keen sight and scent, and strong limbs, he dwells secure amid the loftiest summits, leaping unscathed from crag to crag, up and down the fronts of giddy precipices, crossing foaming torrents and slopes of frozen snow, exposed to the wildest storms, yet maintaining a brave, warm life, and developing from generation to generation in perfect strength and beauty."

Muir caught the essence of the animal nicely, but his prediction of its invulnerability proved dead wrong. Overhunting by miners and competitive grazing by domestic sheep drove bighorn numbers down; by the 1870s, the species had disappeared from the northern Sierra. More than a century later, in 1986, bighorns were reintroduced to Inyo National Forest, east of Yosemite National Park, from a southern Sierra herd.

For most of the last decade, biologist Leslie Chow has monitored those sheep by spotting scope and radio collars. Chow and his colleagues are curious about many things. How do bighorns explore and settle new territory? (Cautiously; ewes with lambs travel very conservatively, while rams are bolder.) What sort of escape terrain do they favor? (Very broken and rough.) What about feeding terrain? (Small wet meadows and seeps, to which they return repeatedly.)

MICHAEL FRYE/EARTHLIGHT

Western cousins of more widespread whitetails, mule deer thrive within many of the West's national forests. Varied habitats of this nationwide system support more than 3,000 wildlife species, including some 283 currently listed as threatened or endangered.

"We only know them by their numbers, but attached to that number is a little bit of personality," Chow told me back in 1990. "You're really happy when one has a lamb. They're kind of our friends. You always look forward to seeing the sheep. It's always exciting."

The bighorn population doubled by the end of the first four years, then doubled again. Then came a crash; the number of sheep observed in Yosemite fell from 89 to 39 in just two years. The harsh winter of 1995 probably had something to do with the decline, and predation by mountain lions and coyotes may have played a part. Chow and his colleagues were bitterly disappointed.

Anyone who has tried against the odds to mend the wing of a hawk or the femur of a raccoon knows something of the bereavement Les Chow felt. Wild creatures are wonderfully tough in their environments, but have a strange fragility outside them. Something happens to wildlife when its connection with the wild is broken. The provision of the National Forests Management Act that requires the Forest Service to maintain viable populations of indigenous animals is a fine one, onerous yet far-sighted. Once a species loses its viability in a particular place, it is often too late. There is something in nature that resists man's attempts to restore the things he has extirpated.

Finding help in human hands, the endangered, red-cockaded woodpecker is returning in force to Florida's Apalachicola National Forest, where a policy of prescribed burning furthers climax stands of longleaf pine—favored by this bird for nest trees. The program has been so successful that Apalachicola birds are used to restock other, depleted forests.

RAYMOND GEHMAN

Fifteen years ago, on a cool, bright day in late September, I stood atop Mount Pinos, in California's Los Padres National Forest, with 20 birders. Most of us wore parkas against the brisk wind blowing over the summit. Below, a badlands of broken ridges stretched away to the west. To the east, dim with haze, lay the southern end of California's San Joaquin Valley. Off to the northwest was the Carrizo Plain. All was condor country. With binoculars we intermittently scanned the sky for the nine-foot wingspan of that great vulture, *Gymnogyps californianus.* Two spotting scopes had been set up on their tripods at the very summit. The priestess at Delphi, I remembered, had delivered her oracles seated on a tripod, and it seemed to me the six legs of the two tripods gave the proceedings on Mount Pinos a vaguely delphic and ceremonial look. We were like one of those misguided sects waiting stubbornly, on high ground, for the end of the world.

In fact we were several sects. John Ogden, of the National Audubon Society and the Condor Recovery Team—an advisory group to the U.S. Fish and Wildlife Service—led a faction that wanted to capture some of the last wild California condors and confine them in zoos in a breeding program. Jerry Emory, former executive director of Golden Gate Audubon, opposed the recovery team and its captive-breeding recommendation. The two men spoke to each other, politely enough, their conversations only slightly strained. There were others from either faction, but the group was mostly rank-and-file bird-watchers, unaligned.

Several golden eagles appeared that morning but no condors, and after several hours of waiting, I slipped away downslope. I found a patch of needle-carpeted ground within a cluster of gnarled Jeffrey pines. The trees cut off the wind, and the needles were sun-warmed. I dozed awhile, then read a paperback, then heard sounds of excitement from the summit and looked around to see a condor passing just below me. It was an adult—I recognized the reddish neck and head. The bird banked slightly, showing white triangles under its wings. I had seen condors on museum trays, dead and desiccated, but never a living one. Behind was a half-mile void—no distance at all for a condor—and then an immature condor, its head still dark, the white blazes under its wings still mottled with dark feathers that fluttered in the wind. Its wings tilted slightly once, twice, then returned to horizontal and never moved again. Condors are so steady in flight that they are routinely mistaken for small planes.

Wind makes a musical whistling in condor pinions, the sound more harmonious in adults than in juveniles, as if the wind-song were something the birds had to learn. These two were too distant for me to hear any music. In my binoculars the dark-headed immature receded smoothly, the wind ceaselessly working the long black "fingers" of its primaries, yet the wings themselves holding motionless. Finally the bird began to shimmy and break up, but this was optical, a result of atmospheric distortion. It occurred to me, as I watched that immature dissolve, that this might represent the last generation of condors; if not the final one before extinction, then the last to fly free.

Gymnogyps californianus is a survivor of an epoch when the scale of life was larger. In the North American Pleistocene, condors waited on musical wings for mammoths to die. They watched mastodons and tapirs struggle in the Rancho La Brea tars. Sometimes on landing, the condors became trapped themselves. Standing in their circles, shuffling and pecking for position, they waited to feed on North American camels, short-faced bears, and lions, on dire wolves and saber-toothed cats. They fled from their giant Pleistocene cousin, *Teratornis*, a bird of 30 pounds or so. *Teratornis* died out with the Pleistocene but *Gymnogyps* survived. As the trend toward miniaturization continues, today's turkey vulture may have the last laugh on the condor.

The captive-breeders eventually won the battle over *Gymnogyps*. All remaining wild condors were captured for breeding in zoos, with the pledge that captive-bred offspring would be released. The anti-capture faction worried that once the condors were caged, their captors would find endless excuses to delay release of any offspring. Time has proved them wrong. Reintroduction began in 1992, and as of this writing, a total of 26 California condors are loose again in the world. They are not exactly "free-flying," as members of the USFWS Condor Recovery Program like to claim, for each wears wing tags and a radio transmitter, and program personnel tend to reel in condors if they detect behavioral problems. But the birds are out there.

The anti-capturists point out that it's hard being a condor. Condor skills—competing with other vultures at carcasses, dodging golden eagles, avoiding power lines—are not easily communicated to hatchlings by the condor-head puppets used in rearing captive birds. Indeed, the first bird to be released drank antifreeze and died, and others have shown a fatal tendency to gravitate to humans in spite of puppet training. No released condors currently at large have yet reached breeding age.

On April 13, 1996, two condors left the Lion Canyon area of Los Padres National Forest and dropped out of radio contact. Field biologists scoured all the obvious places—Santa Barbara, Ventura, and San Luis Obispo counties—for signals but failed. One bird later reappeared at Lion Canyon, while the other eventually was spotted some 250 miles away, near the town of Bishop. That was the farthest that any released condor had ranged. I just happened to arrive at Bishop the same time as that bird. Destiny is peculiar: I drove freely on, while the condor was trapped and transported to a rearing facility. After a few days of observation, it was re-released with the hope it would confine its flights to areas where the Condor Recovery Program believes condors should fly.

The program's biologists have it all wrong, of course. The "missing" condor was not missing at all. Its escape from the network of radio receivers

was not a calamity but a triumph. In flying off the program's monitors it had discovered itself. There is a persistent problem with recovery programs run by the intrusive, hands-on, tranquilize-and-radio-collar school of biology. Its advocates understand what wildness means in their heads, perhaps, but they don't understand with their hearts.

A species is not just genes and flesh and feathers. A species is an interaction between a genetic code and a particular place. A tiger pacing behind bars is not really a tiger. A caged condor is not a condor. Habitat and inhabitant are not a duality but a continuum. Gifford Pinchot, in asserting that national forests should not be preserved as homes for wild creatures, could not have been more wrong. Our national forests have no function more important than as wildlife habitat, as a deep reservoir of genes. It remains to be seen whether those 26 condors reared under artificial conditions will ever learn to be condors indeed. 🌰

Bred in captivity but now flying free, young California condors descend on a stillborn calf placed for their benefit in California's Los Padres National Forest.

FOLLOWING PAGES: *Named for the dean of outdoor photography, Ansel Adams Wilderness includes Thousand Island Lake, in Inyo National Forest.*

Candied by frost, understory vegetation carpets the forest floor of Maroon Bells–Snowmass Wilderness, within Colorado's White River National Forest. Named partly for its massive, red sandstone peaks, this mountained wilderness may remain snowbound for eight or nine months of the year.

Shyness and sharp senses help the desert bighorn survive in Arizona's Tonto National Forest. Diminished by sport hunting and diseases of domestic sheep, the species has retreated to remote areas, often within the national forest system.

FOLLOWING PAGES: Dawn's light finds cloudlike, ethereal fogs adrift over the waters of Redfish Lake, on the edge of Sawtooth Wilderness in Idaho's Sawtooth National Forest.

Backlit by the geologic greenery of Idaho's Vulcan Lake, rough-skinned newts make elegant, eight-inch-long silhouettes amid the Kalmiopsis Wilderness of Siskiyou National Forest. Keeping to dry land for ten months a year, adult

newts live openly in daylight, exuding a skin poison powerful enough to deter most predators except for the naturally immune common garter snake. In early summer, newts migrate to ponds and lakes for courtship and egg laying.

Seemingly transplanted from the Far North, Dolly Sods Wilderness offers lichen-spattered rocks, wind-stunted trees, sphagnum-and-berry bogs, and blazing fall colors—all highly unusual south of the Mason-Dixon line—in West Virginia's botanically diverse Monongahela National Forest.

Seasonal colors also come to lodgepole pines in the West Chichagof–Yakobi Wilderness of Alaska's Tongass National Forest.

FOLLOWING PAGES: *Mirror-image scenics draw visitors to the Maroon Bells–Snowmass Wilderness of Colorado's White River National Forest.*

Named for its raspy call that has been likened to the sound of a saw being sharpened, this northern saw-whet owl—a juvenile—is almost entirely nocturnal. It occurs in various conifer and mixed forests from coast to coast, including but not restricted to the old-growth forests of the Pacific Northwest.

As unpredictable as her brood but far more dangerous, a female Alaskan brown bear brooks no interference as she crosses a grassy meadow in Alaska's Tongass National Forest. Tongass, the largest unit in the national forest system, boasts 17 million acres. America's biggest carnivore, the Alaskan brown bear reaches its greatest size in southern Alaska; males can stand 12 feet tall on the hind legs and weigh up to 1,600 pounds. Cubs may remain with their mothers as long as three or four years before striking out on their own.

Serene majesty of Proxy Falls graces Three Sisters Wilderness, within Oregon's Willamette National Forest, on the glaciered crest of the Cascade Range. Winter snows keep the area inaccessible for seven or eight months a year.

Wilderness and Wildlife

139

Natural camouflage known to biologists as "disruptive coloration" helps this quartet of killdeer eggs evade detection in Montana's Bitterroot National Forest. Adult killdeer rely on feigned broken-wing displays to distract predators and others from their nests.

Momentarily stilled by their own curiosity, red fox pups pause on a ridge in Wyoming's Bighorn National Forest. Intelligent, omnivorous, and adaptable, the species continues to survive almost everywhere in the Northern Hemisphere.

FOLLOWING PAGES: *Dawn mists shroud the forest primeval of Minnesota's Boundary Waters Canoe Area Wilderness, in Superior National Forest.*

Great Outdoors

Forest Service Road 245 in Arizona's Coconino National Forest was slow, sun-baked washboard ahead and clouds of red, talc-fine dust behind. The steering wheel thrummed in my hands as the car vibrated over the washboard and through a hot, resinous parkland of scattered ponderosa pines. Packing in on horseback would have been rougher on the body—but a lot more intimate and fun. I had seen enough ponderosas. Officially, *Pinus ponderosa* occupies about 50,000 square miles of the West, but to those who spend much time here, that estimate can seem way low. The species dominates vast stretches of many southwestern national forests, as well as major chunks of the intermountain, Rocky Mountain, and northwestern regions. Had anyone suggested that day that ponderosas were the most prolific tree in the entire cosmos, I would have believed them. Surely I had taken a wrong turn someplace and was lost on Planet Ponderosa.

"When you've seen one redwood tree, you've seen them all," Ronald Reagan once said. To environmentalists, that philistine observation came to epitomize the old actor's benighted view of things. But in Coconino I had to admit that, at least for ponderosas, *Ronald Reagan was right.*

A short spur road heading off the road to Lava River Cave was an even rougher stretch of washboard. We were happy to leave both dust and car at the trailhead and finish up on foot. Lava River Cave is an old lava tube, created as the margins of a stream of molten rock cooled to form a basaltic shell that insulated the lava within, allowing it to stay liquid. When the last of that lava finally flowed out, a hollow tube was left. Today, the cave's entrance is a dark jumble where the tube's roof collapsed. The refrigerated air flowing from the mouth felt strange and exciting as it cut the heat of the forest. Davey and I zipped up our jackets and descended a short talus slope. Just inside the entrance lay several boulders capped with ice. The air temperature at the cave's entrance holds to about 35°F even when the desert above soars past 100°F. The same insulating properties of basalt that once kept lava molten now keep the cave's subterranean breath cold.

JOEL SARTORE

We were not 30 yards into the cave, flashlight beams traversing the walls, when David's lack of enthusiasm for spelunking became apparent. "What if the lava started flowing right now?" he asked. "We'd be cooked," I conceded, quickly adding that hot lava had not flowed here for ages. I tapped my toe on the rock upon which we stood, a multi-ton block of basalt fallen from the ceiling. "I guess I'd worry more about earthquakes," I said. As we marched deeper into the cave our conversation echoed off the walls, David arguing for retreat, I agreeing in principle but suggesting that we go just a little farther.

About a hundred yards in, I suggested that we turn off our lights to experience total darkness, a blackness blacker than the darkest room or

Backcountry stalwart, 22-year-old Penny still ferries visitors through Idaho's Salmon and Challis National Forests. With countless trails and twice the acreage of national parks, our national forest system serves as a prime outdoor playground.

the most profound, moonless night. We clicked off the flashlights and the blackness pressed in, perfect and unmarred. Not a single photon found its way to us from the outside world. Six seconds of this were enough for Davey. He flicked on his light, reminded me that we had gone "just a little farther" about five times now, and insisted that we start back at once. I gave in. We'd seen no pale, blind salamanders or ghostly crickets or other cave life, nothing but darkness, rocks, and ice. So far, the most fascinating aspect of this cave was that it actually spooked my son. Tree climbing, cliff scaling, outbursts of paternal temper, neighborhood bullies—none had done the job. All it took was a frigid, dark passage into the underworld.

We saw daylight at the end of the lava tube, then suddenly the sun. "Ow!" David complained. "Hurts my eyes." With a hand he shielded his face, like Orpheus returning. Either the sun had exploded into a nova during our absence, or we somehow had emerged onto a different planet. The blazing orb above loomed nearly twice as large as the sun I remembered. The world before us was new and impossibly beautiful. We felt the balmy caress of mountain air, smelled the resinous aroma of ponderosas, heard breezes whisper through pine needles. A moment ago we'd been in a cold and colorless realm—black basalt and the white beams of flashlights. Now light in all its wavelengths flooded Creation. I saw *Pinus ponderosa* as if for the first time: The long, lambent needles, three to a bundle; the soft, warm radiance of the orange-brown bark, fissured into jigsaw-puzzle plates that now seemed to take on some sort of hieroglyphic meaning.

"This species also gives forth the finest music to the wind," John Muir wrote of the ponderosa. "Of all western Pines," Donald Culross Peattie echoed, "this one seems to the beholder most full of light. Its needles, of a rich yellow-green, are burnished like metal. When the shadowless summer winds come plowing through the groves, waving the supple arms and twigs, the long slender needles stream all one way in the current, and the sunlight—astronomically clear and constant—streaks up and down the foliage as from the edge of a flashing sword."

In the past, such ecstatic, Whitmanesque excesses had often caused me to smile. Where, I wondered now, was the excess? Peattie's "flashing sword" was straight reporting. Just 20 minutes underground, and I was seeing the world as Muir and Peattie always seemed to see it, luminous and fresh. If exploring Lava River Cave had been dull, then its aftereffect was alchemy. Like a bite of bread between sips of different vintages, this cave had cleared the palate and made the world new again.

This was truly re-creation, I thought. What a fine word is "recreation," and what a wonderful thing it promises. Too often we have such a drab, weekend-warrior sense of the word—softball games, tennis, fishing poles and beer—but at its roots it means much more. It means nothing less than re-creation: renewal of self and the world.

Through much of its history, the Forest Service resisted recreational use of its lands by the public; Gifford Pinchot's commodity-centered philosophy ruled. In a 1963 speech entitled "Is More Federal Recreation Land Needed?" Charles Gillett of the American Forestry Institute complained sourly that "never before in the history of the United States…has the government had on its payroll so many persons whose job it is to see that the people have fun." That payroll is even larger today. The Forest Service has come to realize that helping people have fun is not an ignoble calling. It is hardly an economic drain, either. USFS projections for the year 2000 anticipate that our national forest lands will generate some $3.5 billion from logging—and a whopping $110.7 billion from recreation, including fishing and hunting revenues. Even so, many Forest Service folk remain reluctant to accept a secondary role for timber.

"I'm not a timber cutter, I'm in recreation," Ken Olsen of Kaibab National Forest told me. "But I personally don't think we cut that much here. The thing is, in my opinion, the environmentalists, they want the national forests to be *national parks*. That's what their goal is. Not, quote, 'hurting' anything. I think for many years the Forest Service probably over-cut some areas. But generally it was for forest health, and for products."

While many forests in the system encourage recreation, some have yet to catch on. In my travels I've often encountered what I consider a kind of user-unfriendliness: poorly marked trails and scarce or even misleading information from ranger offices. FS 245 out to Lava River Cave was one example. Although the Forest Service brochure included a sketch map clearly showing where Highway 180 intersected FS 245, the intersection itself was unmarked. I overshot the turnoff by five miles before realizing something was wrong. Driving back, searching for that all but invisible turnoff, I had to fight the nagging suspicion that the Forest Service, in its collective subconscious, did not really *want* me to find Lava River Cave.

But there are also places like Boundary Waters Canoe Area Wilderness, in Superior National Forest, that are managed for recreation, and managed well. Visitors are limited to groups of nine or fewer, in no more than four watercraft. They must enter where their permits specify, and camp only at designated sites. Apart from a few lakes and rivers that are open to powerboats, most of the area is reserved exclusively for paddlers. Usually I resent restrictions, but not this time. Boundary Waters handles 200,000 people annually; its regulations help minimize human impact and space out the fleets of canoes, allowing everyone a sense of solitude.

Boundary Waters (named for its proximity to the Canadian border) was new country for me. On a five-day canoe trip with photographer Raymond Gehman and his ten-year-old son Andy, I sampled the sort of recreational activities one expects of the North Woods: the meditative rhythms of paddling, bird-watching, fishing for walleye and lake trout and northern pike. But there was another sort of recreation, too, recreation of a terrain and style of life that I had known previously only from books. *The Song of Hiawatha* came to life here. So did *White Falcon*, a boy's novel on the Chippewa that I'd last read when I was Andy's age. It was a pleasure to experience the steady, musical burbling of water under the bow; the ospreys—trim, brown-and-white birds as neat as their jumbled stick nests were untidy; the raucous gulls and ravens that hung about camp; the welcome squadrons of dragonflies that dispersed the mosquitoes; the long-legged wolf spiders, poised on shoreline logs and ready to pursue prey underwater; the eerie calls and comic, lunatic dances of the loons.

It may sound perverse, but I discovered here that I enjoyed portaging as much as paddling. Pull on a backpack heavy with food or gear, heave a canoe over your head, and trudge under that 17-foot-long cap—heart pounding, sweat rolling, lungs pumping like bellows—up over the granite dome of yet another divide and down to the far shore, and you know you are alive. I loved the way that the canoe's long brim forced my attention downward, acquainting me with details I might otherwise have missed: glacial scars on the granite; wolf scat full of hair and the bony fragments of deer; spruce seedlings colonizing stony cracks; bunchberries and wood anemones and wild roses growing thick along trail margins. Portages are measured in rods. This antiquated unit remains useful here because it roughly equals a canoe length. After making a portage of 130 or 150 or 200 rods, I felt stronger, not weaker; it almost seemed that I had recreated a younger version of myself.

Recreation itself is creative, and new forms of it continually appear within our national forests. One relatively new wrinkle involves volunteer programs—participants assist biologists with their wildlife research or help restore historic buildings on forest lands, for example. Another twist offers overnight stays at fire towers and other unusual sites, for a fee.

Every February in Osceola National Forest, recreation takes the form of reenactment as Civil War buffs from all across the nation gather to refight the Battle of Olustee, Florida's biggest military encounter. In February, 1864, Union troops attempting to cut off Florida from the rest of the Confederacy met Rebel forces under General Joseph Finegan amid the pines of what is now Osceola National Forest.

"This is a battle that people down here like, because the Confederacy won," a female ranger at Osceola's interpretive center told me. She added that there was an attraction for Northerners, too: At a skirmish before the main battle, the Union won.

Eric Hague of Lake Geneva, Florida, has been a reenactor since 1984, traveling from one Civil War battle site to another, an itinerant hired gun shooting blanks. "When we go to a reenactment," he told me, "we ask the people who put on the event, what do you need? When they say they need more Union, we go Union. At Olustee, we go 15th U.S. Regular Army, and then our counterpart is Company D, 1st Florida."

"So you don't mind fighting for the Yankees?" I asked.

Hague laughed. "Well, I tell my Southern counterparts I die quickly. Besides, my ancestors were on the Confederate and Union sides, both."

"Have you ever been tempted to change history and fight Olustee to a different conclusion?"

GEORGE WUERTHNER

Paddlers pause at Sunflower Hot Springs, beside the Middle Fork of Idaho's Salmon River. Boat-slamming white water punctuates this 100-mile torrent as it twists through a steep gorge in Salmon and Challis National Forests.

"No, no, no!" cried Hague. "You got to go by the book. We camp authentic wherever we go. As the war years go on, the gear changes. I myself have a wall tent which is Early War, and I can deck it out completely. Later, I go into an A-frame, which I can deck out in that time period. Then, in Late War, we use a kind of a shelter-half for the Confederates. For the Union it's still the A-frame. Even your clothing changes. Good Lord, I have one closet full of uniforms according to the battle and the style of the period. And of course we have the weapons. We load from 30 to 60 grains of gunpowder, and we pre-roll the gunpowder, and we put it in our cartridge box, and we sit around and talk about the different styles of bullets they had, even back then. Either the third or the sixth shot they fired out of the Enfield or Springfield was a cleaning round, and we'll argue about that. That's how technical we get."

At Olustee and other battles, Eric Hague has died a thousand deaths. Sometimes a reenactor's fate is determined by draw. Sometimes death comes whenever he runs out of ammunition. Sometimes his commander orders him to drop, usually when artillery fires. "It's a turn-on for the artillery men to just see you fall down," Hague explained. He added that a soldier who falls during an advance can rise up again in retreat once the fleeing troops are around him, making his resurrection less noticeable. In all his reenactments of the Battle of Olustee—where opposing forces advance and retreat three times—Hague has lived more lives than a cat.

Death can be sweet, he admitted. "Especially in the Battle of Atlanta. We had to go around a mountain to get to the rear of the Union troops. We were exhausted. When we got to the battlefield, half of us in the first charge went down. We didn't *want* to come back to life."

The unending Battle of Olustee, fought over and over again in commemoration of ancestors, is recreation of the finest sort. From under the brims of their caps, in respite from the fake battle and the real struggles of their personal lives, the fallen troops, Union and Confederate, gaze up through the needles of longleaf pines into the blue of the Florida sky.

Recreation can involve not only unconventional activities but also some pretty unconventional participants. More than 16 years ago, in California's Stanislaus National Forest, I ran its namesake river with an outfit called Environmental Traveling Companions, which focused on introducing handicapped people to white water. I am nominally whole and sound of body but had been invited along anyway. At dusk on the eve of the trip, amid wild oats and pines of the Sierra Nevada foothills, I watched a dove calling. I turned to Kit Chan Lau, a blind Social Security worker from Berkeley.

"You hear that?" I asked her. "That's a dove."

"I know it's a dove." She was staring heavenward, listening. "I know the sound of an owl, too. In China, if you hear an owl early in the morning,

Swathed in solitude, a lone fisherman works man-made Kincaid Lake, at the headwaters of Bayou Beous in Louisiana's Kisatchie National Forest. Fishing's huge appeal has prompted the Forest Service to develop spawning beds and stabilize channels in numerous forests.

it's a bad sign. Owls call when somebody dies or something bad happens."

Kit had been born outside Canton, she told me. She had measles at the age of one, and for five days her eyes stayed closed. When her aunt finally forced Kit's eyelids apart, the eyes were all white, with just the pale, bluish moons of irises and the faintest trace of pupils.

Early the next morning we drove to the river. Trip leader Mark DuBois and two boatmen had preceded us, setting out three inflatable rafts on the riverbank. We pumped them up until the gray neoprene was tight, then slid them into the river, and began loading gear. Walking raftward with waterproof dunnage bags, I looked up to see an attractive blonde in jeans descending the stony slope above. At her feet crawled a burly man, or five-eighths of one. Both legs were missing at the hips. His left arm was gone below the elbow, and a black patch covered his right eye. Propelled by his good arm, which was brawny, and by a wiggling of hips, he slid over the stones in a sitting position, moving about as fast as a whole person strolls. His hair was reddish and curly; a scar ran from cheek to jaw. The partial man brought a strange excitement with him, radiating ego and confidence. There was a swagger in his crawl, if that is possible.

The woman was Jeri Burnotte. The legless man was her husband, Jim, who trained horses for a living and taught handicapped people to ride and swim. A year or two earlier, Jim Burnotte had been named Mr. Handicapped America. He'd been Mr. Handicapped California before that, and Mr. Handicapped Colorado when he lived in that state. Back in October of 1968 he'd been Specialist Fourth Class Jim Burnotte, a 21-year-old army MP serving in Vietnam. He was driving a jeep when the Viet Cong detonated a 105-mm shell they'd buried under the road. His best friend, on the seat beside him, died instantly; Jim became a triple amputee. One eye was destroyed, his jaw was broken, his remaining arm mangled. It took 25 operations to piece him together again. Today, despite the cool morning air, his only top was a T-shirt.

"Did you bring wool clothes?" Mark asked him.

"Don't need them," Jim answered. "I always overheat. My heart pumps enough blood for a whole human body, and there's only half of me here."

The Stanislaus was the busiest small river I'd ever seen. Neoprene rafts were loading up and leaving shore by the dozen, some propelled by a single oarsman sitting amidships. Others, including ours, were paddle rafts in which passengers sit along the pontoons and follow instructions from a coxswain in the stern.

We pushed off, caught the current, and spun lazily downstream through a gorge several hundred feet deep. The canyon's steep walls were golden with wild oats. Here and there grew live oaks and foothill pines. I saw an occasional squirrel and one muskrat track, but what most animated this landscape was the living river.

It took a while to get the hang of paddle boating. "Right turn!" our boatman would yell. We'd all think a moment, then most starboard-siders would backpaddle while most port-siders would paddle forward—with a few daydreamers getting it wrong and going against the grain. But after two or three rapids, we managed to smooth out our raggedness and obey orders automatically, mindlessly.

Watching Kit Lau's face as we went through several rapids, I gradually realized that water that looks bad doesn't always *sound* bad. She smiled happily all the way through a chute that to me seemed horrible, yet as we neared a mild-looking riffle, a shadow of anxiety darkened her face. We rounded a bend, and a new rapid was upon us, the scariest looking yet. "Whooossh," said Kit, gaily imitating the sibilance of the very water that to me seemed so ominous. Poised on a V-shaped tongue of smooth water

CAROL & ED MACKAY/F-STOCK, INC.

Chilling out in a sudden summer squall, mountain bikers make an unscheduled stop on their tour of Idaho's Salmon and Challis National Forests, prized for rugged peaks and canyons, for mirror lakes and ghost towns that date to the boom days of gold mining.

that led to the rapid's heart, we entered an instant of suspended time. Then, with all of us yelling, the rapid sucked us into its roar and tumult.

Curtis Wilson, who suffers from cerebral palsy, clung to a strap through the rough stuff, like a rodeo rider atop a Brahma bull. As we drifted in slack water later, I asked him if this was his first white-water experience. "Yes, first," he answered, after a moment of lag time. His blue eyes were full of humor but a smile was sometimes difficult to arrange, and his speech was a recording played at the wrong speed. "How do you like it?" I asked. Curtis's face gathered itself. "Gr·r·reat!" he roared, sounding like Tony the Tiger in a Frosted Flakes commercial. His face gathered again. "Of course, if I had fallen in, I might feel different."

Everyone laughed. Curtis's requisite pauses had the same effect as a professional comedian's timing, making us hang on every word and listen hard for what was next. He was always joking; his delayed, Jack Bennyesque delivery made his routines funny even when the lines were awful.

A river has a powerful way of manufacturing community. Here we were jammed together on tiny rafts, united by a lot of fun and a little danger. It is remarkable how quickly, on a river, a group of humans becomes a tribe. By evening, as we sat in a circle on the bank after dinner, we were better friends—more familiar in our language, taking greater liberties—than our brief acquaintance gave us any right to be.

The next morning, Mark DuBois gave a crash course in kayaking. Kit was his first pupil. Standing beside her in shallow water, he began by asking her to run her hand around the rim of the paddling hole and then feel the seat. He showed her how the paddle shaft, held crosswise against the deck, would serve as stabilizing brace while she lowered herself in. Then he explained how the paddle's twin blades were set at 90° angles to each other, and guided her hands through the proper motions.

It seemed too brief to me. Did Kit understand the 90° angles? The kayak itself was a bad fit: Mark stood six feet eight; Kit not quite five feet. Her toes barely reached the knee braces of his kayak, and the paddle was much too long. Kayaks roll easily. What would Kit do if she suddenly found herself upside-down and underwater?

She set off, alone but smiling, into what was for her a river of total darkness. Jim Burnotte shook his head. "Can you imagine how scary that is?" he asked. "I'd be scared to death."

Kit did fairly well, though whenever she left dead water for the edge of a current, she tended to turn in circles. "You're going good!" Jim shouted encouragement. After ten minutes on the river, still smiling, she paddled confidently back toward the beacon of our voices.

Jim went next. Doubtful that the stump of his left arm could handle the tricky rotation of the kayak paddle, he opted for a canoe paddle.

Jim Burnotte had the worst possible build for kayaking. Nearly all his weight was topside in his burly torso; hardly any was below deck. With one arm gone, his weight was out of balance as well. Still, he was determined to try. He took a single stroke, the kayak rolled, and the Vietnam vet disappeared under the water.

When Mark reached out to right the kayak, Jim came up grinning, spitting water, and shouting to Kit, "I already went in the water! And I haven't even left shore." Almost immediately, Jim set out again. Whatever he'd done wrong the first time, he'd learned. He never rolled the kayak again. Somehow, from the very start of his second try, he mastered a J-stroke that kept the boat in a straight line. He played for a while in the current, then returned to shore and traded the canoe paddle for the double-bladed kayak paddle. Grasping the shaft in his right hand and in the crook of his left elbow, he figured out the proper rotation. He took scarcely two or three

Rising above traditional tenting, these campers in Oregon's Siskiyou National Forest dine and overnight high atop Pearsoll Peak in a restored, 1954 fire lookout. This and other lookouts, rendered obsolete by fire-spotting planes, have found new life as units for rent.

RAYMOND GEHMAN

strokes to master it, then shot the kayak out into the main current.

Watching him fly in the kayak, I realized that this white-water trip was as challenging for us, the sound of body, as it was for the crippled. Everyone is flawed in some way—as our handicapped companions would sometimes remind us, gently. Running the Stanislaus with people like Jim and Kit and Curtis was an inspiring lesson in the transcendence of the human spirit. It expanded our sense of our own possibilities.

Laughing fiercely, Jim drove the kayak across a stretch of fast water. For him, recreation was more than fun; it was a continuing and heroic act of reconstruction. He never ceased reshaping the half of himself that survived his terrible wounding. That day, he remade himself as a kayaker.

Many years later, hiking through sand pines of the Florida scrub in Ocala National Forest, I came to a sign for Juniper Prairie Wilderness.

Life imitates art: Curious raccoon in Ocala National Forest mimics a scene from The Yearling, *Marjorie Kinnan Rawlings's story of life in a Florida pine forest. The real-life family that inspired her novel finds eternal rest in Pats Island cemetery (opposite).*

The sign had been split by vandals or the weather, and its decayed state was fine with me. The fewer signs of man in a designated wilderness, the better. I set off down a white-sand path. My goal, Pats Island—as that slight rise of tall pines amid the Florida scrub is grandly called—was the setting for Marjorie Kinnan Rawlings's fictional classic *The Yearling*. I was headed there as a kind of homage.

The trail soon left the sand pines for a big burn of longleaf pines, then petered out after two miles. Cursing the Forest Service for not marking things better—the agency can't win with people like me—I backtracked and found what I hoped was the true trail. Palmettos gave way to grass prairies pocked with ponds that boiled with minnows. Scrub jays looked down from the pines. A redbird crossed the trail like a flaming arrow. A fat young raccoon ran from me and scuttled up a pine. I neared the tree and the coon shinnied higher. Its black mask failed to hide the mix of fear and curiosity with which it regarded me.

Suddenly a shock of recognition. I recalled words I'd read just the night before, in *The Yearling*. "A half-grown raccoon was peering around

the side of the trunk, a dozen feet from the ground. It saw itself observed and pulled back out of sight. In an instant the masked face looked again." Here was recreation of another sort: life imitating art. The art of a careful observer like Rawlings had been drawn in turn from life. I scribbled "treed coon" in my notebook—and the animal entered art again. Recreation reverberated in a short feedback loop amid the Florida scrub.

Fifty yards down the trail from the raccoon, I met the first humans I had encountered that day, a man from Gainesville with two small sons, breaking for lunch beside a prairie pond. "Call it 46 hours, guys," the man was saying, consulting his watch. "It's been that long since we've seen anybody." We parted ways, and for the rest of the day I saw no one else.

But on Pats Island I found the cemetery where Reuben Long and his family, the real-life inspiration for the fictional Baxters of *The Yearling*, had been buried (above). I encountered a few ghosts among the tombstones, conversed with a red-shouldered hawk who, like most of his kind, complained continually. Then I walked slowly back, feeling fulfilled. 🌰

FOLLOWING PAGES: Sunlight, limestone formations, and the crystalline waters of Alexander Springs work their magic on a young snorkeler in Ocala, site of numerous swimming holes. Pure Florida aquifer water, at a constant 72°F, feeds this and other sites.

Winter fashions flare above legendary Sun Valley, in Idaho's Sawtooth National Forest. Like many U.S. ski areas, Sun Valley leases forest lands, an arrangement that channels revenues to the Forest Service as well as to local economies.

FOLLOWING PAGES: *Shooting a rapid named Pipeline, a kayaker takes on the Wild and Scenic Lochsa River in Idaho's Clearwater National Forest. Icy waters and cool air temperatures make hypothermia a constant concern.*

Fostering "alternative vacations"—and generous doses of community spirit—
the USFS Passport in Time program puts volunteers to work on backcountry
projects that range from archaeology to surveying to replacing the roof (top and
above) on a historic ranger station in Montana's Gallatin National Forest.

Historic preservation specialist Bernie Weisgerber (above) uses old-time tools and methods in Gallatin, his recipe for assuring authenticity of restoration efforts. FOLLOWING PAGES: *Skiing Big Sky country, a touring enthusiast glides a ridgeline of Montana's Beartooth Mountains, in Custer National Forest.*

PORTFOLIO BY RAYMOND GEHMAN

Superior National Forest

Capped by his canoe, a visitor to Superior's Boundary Waters Canoe Area
Wilderness portages through dense North Woods awash in swirls of leaf-filtered

light as he follows the footsteps of 18th-century voyageurs. Composed of mostly roadless, lake-dappled miles along the U.S.-Canada border, *Boundary Waters* ranks as the nation's most popular designated wilderness, drawing 200,000 people yearly. Natural terrain and a strict, efficient permit system help ensure a quality wilderness experience for all, complete with loon laughs and wolf howls.

Only a two-day paddle from roadhead, Cherry Lake (above) lies relatively near civilization. Some visitors spend weeks seeking more remote and even more pristine sanctuaries islanded with towering pines and spruce. With few exceptions, Boundary Waters bans the use of motors, sails, portage wheels—even canned food. Purists exult in the transcendent attractions of nature untamed, of daily rhythms keyed to the sun's arc and the paddle's dip. Local wildlife ranges from dragonfly (opposite) to snapping turtle, from moose to mink, from lake trout to loon; these and other creatures give visitors reason to idle—and to experience, if only fleetingly, another place and time.

FOLLOWING PAGES: Shimmering, band-of-gold sunset lingers at Elbow Lake.

Great Outdoors

The Future

. . . .

A phalanx of huge saguaros stood at roadside, 700 strong, close-ranked against the distant blue of the Superstition Mountains. High on each cactus was a yoke of red rubber, from which three guy ropes ran tautly down to the ground. Saguaros are surreal plants, improbable enough just growing wild in the desert. But here, massed together and restrained, they seemed positively otherworldly, like 700 vegetable Gullivers tethered by Lilliputians. Their pleated crowns bore rows of green buds, some of which had blossomed creamy white. Nearby stood squat rows of barrel cactuses and a leafless, thorny forest of ocotillos. The ocotillos flowered scarlet, while hummingbirds flew precision routes among the thorns.

The Arizona Department of Transportation, in widening a stretch of Highway 87 through Tonto National Forest, had displaced this desert flora and, in compliance with Forest Service requirements, had created a temporary storage "nursery" for them here. Once the highway was complete, all the cactuses and ocotillos would be replanted along it.

Here, it seemed to me, was a fine example of sensitivity within the Forest Service. There was a time when road builders just leveled whatever stood in their way. But today, seeing these rescued plants flowering in captivity, I felt a surge of hope for the future.

Howard Ludwig showed me around. Employed by a contractor for the road project, Ludwig is a database programmer pressed into cactus duty. He cheerfully admitted that only five months earlier, all he "knew about cactus was that you didn't want to back into one." But now, after poring over books and quizzing botanists, he fairly bristled with cactus knowledge. He had compiled information on each of the thousands of cactuses in the nursery, and had set up a database program to field new information. He pointed out some stress signs for saguaros. Here were gray scars left by passing fires. There were shrunken pleats—usually evidence of drier-than-normal times. When a plant is already stressed, Ludwig and his colleagues grow nervous about moving it.

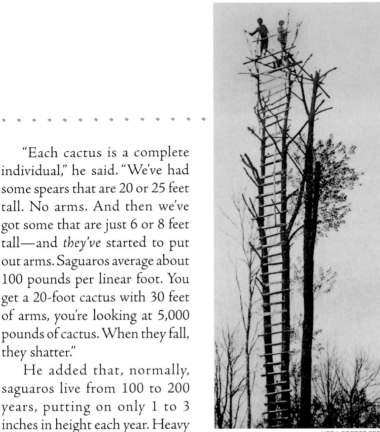

USDA FOREST SERVICE

"Each cactus is a complete individual," he said. "We've had some spears that are 20 or 25 feet tall. No arms. And then we've got some that are just 6 or 8 feet tall—and *they've* started to put out arms. Saguaros average about 100 pounds per linear foot. You get a 20-foot cactus with 30 feet of arms, you're looking at 5,000 pounds of cactus. When they fall, they shatter."

He added that, normally, saguaros live from 100 to 200 years, putting on only 1 to 3 inches in height each year. Heavy rains can cause them to expand so fast that they actually split. Ludwig stopped before a big saguaro to pluck at one of its spines. The *plick* he produced was almost musical.

Early lookout tower in West Virginia made a precarious perch for spotting fires—a chore now performed largely by aerial patrols. Also updated: the belief that fire and forests don't mix. Foresters today realize that fires are both natural and necessary to a healthy ecosystem.

"One of the functions of the spines is to prevent the wind from evaporating moisture," he said. "When the wind blows, these things whistle and howl. The spines help form a dead air-space between the ribs, and they provide a certain amount of shade for the skin."

A dark hollow pocked one cactus. I stuck my hand inside, and the interior of the spear was almost frigid. "The whole thing is water cooled," said Ludwig, explaining that within its tough, dry, waxy exterior, each saguaro has a core of osmotic tissue that pumps water up its trunk and arms. "That's why woodpeckers build their houses in them."

Galen Drake, a landscape architect involved with the project, joined us. "We're all going through a learning curve here," Drake said. "At the beginning, nobody had a feel for the sheer magnitude of the cactus operation. The more everybody got into it, the more overwhelming it became."

But their experiences here also enabled them to break new ground. Traditionally, Drake said, transplanters had buried the bottom two or three feet of a big saguaro, for stability. The Tonto team discovered that this actually puts the root system too deep to get sufficient water, and increases the risk of the trunk rotting. They found that too much root was being left behind, and they made adjustments. They also devised an antidote for rot: streptomycin spray, followed by a dusting of sulfur.

I noticed, low on the trunk of each nursery saguaro, a white smear of spray paint. I asked what it signified. "That's the north-side spot," Ludwig said. "Only in midsummer does sun hit the northern exposure of a cactus. It gets so acclimated to its position that if you turn the north side to the south, it gets sunburned! The south side is accustomed to the sun. It gets hardened to sunlight. The ribs on the south side grow closer together."

Later, as we surveyed the captive, stubby-armed army one more time, Ludwig said, "There's a hell of a lot of pride out here. There was a lot of work done. Right here in the nursery, there's 700 saguaros we've saved." Six months down the road, that number would swell to 1,200.

And yet, even as the Forest Service lavishes almost extravagant care on Tonto's cactuses, it sanctions clear-cutting in Alaska's magnificent Tongass National Forest. Tongass, by far the system's largest forest—a global treasure—has been subjected to ruinous timber practices. We fault South Americans for the destruction of Amazonia, yet our own rain forest is also in danger and is disappearing before our eyes.

The Tongass Timber Reform Act of 1990 was designed to correct decades of abuse in the Tongass. But according to a report by the Association of Forest Service Employees for Environmental Ethics, the Forest Service violated this law both in letter and in spirit: The agency allowed the biggest and rarest stands to be logged out of proportion to their natural occurrence, contrary to a provision of the act. It also failed, in places, to enforce the minimum 100-foot, no-cut buffer zones required along all salmon and high-quality trout streams. And it ignored scientific studies that recommended reduced cutting to protect certain wildlife.

Spokesmen at Tongass today deny any wrongdoing and disparage the report's claims. But numerous field biologists and others who know this forest insist that areas with higher quality trees *have* been cut at too rapid a rate. Many also note that Tongass sells its timber to logging companies at a net loss to the taxpayer. Most timber sales throughout all national forests lose money; they are not sales as much as subsidies for the timber industry. But no forest runs more red ink than Tongass. In 1992 its timber programs ran up the biggest annual loss for any forest in history: over $64 million, according to the Native Forest Council; $42 million, according to the federal government's General Accounting Office.

Surely the Forest Service has a split personality, born of endless conflict between good policies and egregiously bad ones. Large stretches of Florida's Apalachicola National Forest, for example, are being managed for the benefit of red-cockaded woodpeckers. This forest now produces enough "excess" birds to restock other national forests—a success story. But in the Sierra Nevada, the selfsame Forest Service has been embroiled in controversy over the cutting of old-growth habitat vital to California spotted owls and other wildlife. The agency also increased recommended levels of logging for all ten national forests in the Sierra, from a total of 416 million board feet a year to 620 million. This, despite findings by its own biologists that showed population models for owls decreasing annually between 1990 and 1995, despite a 1996 report of the Sierra Nevada Ecosystem Project linking destructive logging practices to the decline of the Sierra ecosystem. On the day the San Francisco office of the USFS was set to propose this new revision, the White House intervened and called for scientific review.

In one Sierran national forest, Eldorado, Forest Service managers approved 24 timber sales during the late 1980s and early 1990s. But in 1993, new information relating to the environment prompted Eldorado's newly appointed supervisor to suspend those sales. This flip-flop may cost taxpayers as much as $30 million, since timber companies are suing for breach of contract. Already the affair has proved costly to morale: It's been reported that Forest Service biologists and others were pressured to alter findings and falsify documents in order to speed approvals.

Being a government forester is not an easy life. Few federal agencies are more maligned than the Forest Service, and the agency is constantly besieged by interest groups at opposite ends of the political spectrum.

"There are highly consumptive groups on one extreme," John Kramer of Gila National Forest told me, "and some preservationists on the other extreme. These extremes each represent maybe 10 percent of the people.

We're not hearing from the 80 percent in the middle. Sometimes a small specialty group will win a lawsuit; we'll swing management in that direction. Then the other side, three years later, will win a lawsuit, and we'll swing it that way. That's no way to be managing national forests."

The agency's ongoing dilemma was personified by the resignation of Jack Ward Thomas as chief of the Forest Service late in 1996. Thomas, the first wildlife biologist ever to head the agency, proved ill-equipped for Washington politics and found himself caught in the cross fire generated by loggers, environmentalists, and factions within his own agency.

"He's too brown for much of the environmental movement and too green for the timber industry," says Tim Hermach, executive director of the Native Forest Council. It is a diagnosis that fits the Forest Service itself.

Historian Alfred Runte wrote, "A common expression within the Forest Service goes something like this: If everyone is mad at me some of the time, then I must be doing my job, for if anyone is always satisfied, then I am probably giving that person too much."

RAYMOND GEHMAN

Some old ways remain the best: At historic Ninemile Remount Depot in Montana's Lolo National Forest, forest rangers learn the time-honored techniques of mule packing— still often the most practical means of getting into the roadless backcountry.

In forest after forest, I heard variations on this basic theme. Cecelia Dargan, a wildlife specialist in Coconino National Forest, told me, "We're an agency that has to mesh an awful lot of values, so we probably should be pretty much in the middle. You're not going to make everybody happy, but that's all right as long as nobody's screaming too loud."

This formula has a democratic ring and seems to make sense. But the state of America's forests today and the challenges ahead all argue against a middling path. In national forests of the northern Rockies, already many watersheds are marginal or degraded. Since the 1980s, chip mills have been springing up across the country. They rely almost entirely on clear-cutting; they target trees of ever-smaller diameter, threatening to further abbreviate harvest cycles that some warn are already too short. In the Sierra Nevada, foresters report a gradual increase in ozone injury among pines. Ponderosas in San Bernadino National Forest suffer from various pests and air pollution. Eastern flowering dogwoods are dying across widespread areas of the Appalachians, especially above 3,000 feet. The gypsy moth, an introduced pest currently established in 17 states, defoliates millions of acres of hardwoods yearly.

Carrying a cargo of tradition, a mixed packtrain of mules and horses wends its way into Lolo's backcountry on an overnight training exercise out of Ninemile Remount Depot. Today's Forest Service seeks to blend the best of old and new as it heads into its second century.

RAYMOND GEHMAN

Lifelong forester Gordon Robinson came up with a credo far better, I think, than the hew-to-the-middle trend so popular now. Gordon knows both sides of the timber debate; after 27 years as chief forester for the Southern Pacific Land Company, he became forestry consultant to the Sierra Club. In a published interview he said, "Foresters should be loyal to—the forest—their own profession. They should not be employees; they should be able to say to their clients, 'I'm sorry, but what you want to do is inconsistent with good forest practices. If you want to do that, you'll have to get someone else.' And any forester who would go along with unethical practices should be subject to prosecution in some manner. I just think we've got to separate foresters from businessmen."

Today there is a growing movement to end logging in national forests. The Native Forest Council argues for such a "zero-cut" policy; so does the membership of the Sierra Club. Many Americans believe there should be *no* commercial resource extraction on public lands, neither oil-drilling nor mining nor logging.

"It's time for the Forest Service to abandon its role as a producer of commodities," environmentalists John Baden and Pete Geddes contend on the op-ed page of the *Wall Street Journal*. "The agency should focus its considerable expertise on the protection of wilderness and wildlife and the promotion of recreation and research in national forests. Commodity production is best left to the private sector."

Zero-cut might set Gifford Pinchot to spinning in his grave, but not much faster than he is already—for less than 15 percent of America's lumber currently comes from our national forests. Most is in private hands.

My environmentalist father argues for a better way to assess the worth of trees. "The marketplace," he reasons, "gives a value only for the pulp you can get out of a tree, or the two-by-fours. The marketplace says nothing about the value of trees for their locking up carbon dioxide and liberating oxygen, producing soil and keeping it in place, capturing and storing solar energy, some of it for millennia, providing habitat for millions of species, most of them not yet discovered. The marketplace says nothing at all about the beauty of the forest. All those things are missed by the marketplace— and are a measure of its incompetence."

In the Forest Service as in other governmental agencies, change rarely is rapid. But it is possible. One example is the fairly recent shift from relentless fire-suppression to prescribed burnings. Conflagrations like the Yellowstone fire have shown how the old, suppress-every-fire policy can lead to accumulation of dangerous levels of fuel.

Gray F. Reynolds, deputy chief of the Forest Service, notes other changes as well: "There has been increasing emphasis on ecosystems, on the incorporation of new scientific information into decision making, and on a reduction in the use of traditional timber management techniques. Increasing emphasis is being placed on the protection of critical habitat for a variety of species; on air, water, and visual quality; on fuel and fire hazard reduction; on recreational opportunities; and on the sustainability of biological and human communities. National forest system lands and resources will continue to be managed in new and adaptive ways to meet the needs of those resources and the American people."

The agency's new chief, Michael Dombeck, who is a biologist as well as the former acting director of the Bureau of Land Management, is also optimistic on where the Forest Service is headed into the next century. His first priority, he said, "is to build on the rich tradition of working closely with local communities to restore and maintain productive, healthy, and diverse ecological systems. Effective stewardship begins and ends in the community. As managers of the public trust, our job is to ensure

Hands-on training for tomorrow's resource managers: At the Nature High Summer Camp in Utah's Fishlake National Forest, USFS Ranger Max Reid shows students how to translate core borings of trees into local histories of environmental conditions.

RAYMOND GEHMAN

that all who use the land—be they anglers, timber companies, or hikers—support the land's conservation and restoration."

Perhaps our national forests should become, once again, the people's forests. Too many have been managed as if they belonged to the timber industry. Gifford Pinchot envisioned forests that would stand in shining contrast to lands devastated by abusive timbering practices; they were to be exemplars of enlightened forestry. We need to realize that ideal.

Late one spring, following what had been the snowiest winter in years, I drove my son up into the White Mountains of Inyo National Forest, hoping to show him something my father had once shown me. Part of the Sierra Nevada, Inyo harbors—among other things—*Pinus longaeva*, Great Basin bristlecone pines. One local patriarch called the "Methuselah Tree" has 4,723 rings—making it the oldest known living tree on earth.

Snow still blocked some roads, but we managed to drive to within two miles of our goal before setting off on foot. The road twisted steeply up a desert mountainside of sage and widely scattered piñon pines. We were at 10,000 feet. Gradually the piñons gave way to an occasional young bristlecone, its crown all brushy with green foxtails. At such tender age, *Pinus longaeva* is full of life but is not particularly distinguished, giving no hint of the wonder it will become.

Ancient bristlecones are mostly dead, alive only in a thin ribbon of bark and a few green branches, yet the bare, golden contortions of their deadwood are surpassingly beautiful. Their squat trunks are gnarled and whorly; their short, twisty branches are all wild, operatic gesture. It is hard to miss their lesson of persistence in the face of adversity. They root in arid, alkaline soil; they branch in the thin air and harsh ultraviolet light of high altitude; their growth is stunted. The harsher the conditions, the slower the growth—and the more twisted and beautiful the form. The slowest-growing ones produce dense wood impregnated with resins that make it so resistant to rot and disease that it can endure for many centuries even after the tree dies. It is these tough and tortured individuals that are likeliest to join the oligarchy of the quadrimillennials.

In fact, bristlecones are loveliest *after death*. Once the distraction of their needles is gone, they become pure sculpture, their lifeless wood billowing out of gray granite like fossilized flames. They do not decay like lesser trees; they erode as stone erodes, imperceptibly, scoured and polished by centuries of windblown sand. A grove of them is less like a conventional forest than like a stand of ruined stelae in the desert.

That night we camped amid piñon pines at 8,500 feet, just below the zone of the bristlecones. After dinner we were studying the star-jammed sky when the brightest meteor I have ever seen streaked, brilliant green, across the entire arc of heaven. How many thousands of meteors, I wondered, had the Methuselah Tree witnessed during its 4,723 years? In its recollections—if a bristlecone has recollections—the sky must be scribbled with meteor trails, like time exposures of city traffic at night.

It struck me that this tree's name is a diminishing metaphor. The biblical Methuselah lived 969 years—scarcely past infancy in bristlecone time. Some oaks live nearly that long. Inyo's Methuselah Tree sprouted during the early days of Sumer; it was a mere sapling when Gilgamesh felled the cedars of Mesopotamia. It gained size even as the great monuments at Karnak were rising. It has witnessed the arrival of Buddhism,

Christianity, Islam, Impressionism, Expressionism, dialectical materialism. What else might it yet see in its lifetime? Here, it seemed to me, was the model. We need a forest system with the steadiness of its oldest trees. We need a system dedicated to truly sustainable harvests—or no harvests—a system run by principled foresters tough enough to resist fads and bad ideas.

"There has been a fundamental misconception," Gifford Pinchot once argued, "that conservation means nothing but the husbanding of resources for future generations. There could be no more serious mistake."

Ah, but I—and many others—believe we must make that "mistake" repeatedly, and with passion. We need a national forest system good for the ages, because the ages lie ahead. 🌰

Dead but not departed, the woody remains of millennia-old bristlecone pines—extremely resistant to rot—persevere in California's Inyo National Forest.

FOLLOWING PAGES: *New seedlings and saplings begin to fill in a recent clear-cut in Washington State's Olympic National Forest. Beyond, relatively uniform stands indicate older clear-cuts that have regenerated more completely, bearing testimony to the principle of sustainable harvest.*

Looking like lassoed aliens, blooming saguaros—stabilized by guy ropes— survive temporary transplantation during road construction in Arizona's Tonto National Forest. Eventually, they will be replanted along the route.

FOLLOWING PAGES: *Lightning-spawned fires scorch ponderosa pines and Douglas firs in Tonto National Forest. Frequent, quick-racing "healthy" fires keep flammable debris from building up, and rarely harm mature trees.*

Clear-cutting and clear water seem a side-by-side reality in this eight-year-old photograph of Gifford Pinchot National Forest (above)—but a downpour can turn such exposed areas into instant torrents of mud. Indeed, catastrophic mudslides now plague parts of the Pacific Northwest. Loggers today must hew to stricter guidelines than their predecessors, including observance of no-cut buffer zones along all surface streams. For its part, the agency uses controlled burns to reduce logging debris (opposite) and deter the spread of wildfires.

FOLLOWING PAGES: During a controlled burn in a sequoia stand in California, researchers use temperature probes to determine heat intensity nearly two feet down. Underground temperatures above 147°F kill root systems. Near-total exclusion of fires means buildup of debris—and hotter, more destructive fires.

Gaunt signs of ecosystem woes, dead Jeffrey pines on Lake Tahoe's shore (above) succumbed to a widespread infestation of bark beetles, which burrow into each tree's vital cambium layer (opposite, top). Such trees pose a fire hazard, exacerbated by recent drought. A remotely operated submersible (opposite, bottom) explores a 6,000-year-old pine forest on lake bottom—evidence that Tahoe's level was then far below its current mark. Three national forests— Tahoe, Eldorado, and Toiyabe—rim this lake on the California-Nevada border.

FOLLOWING PAGES: In Florida's Apalachicola National Forest, prescribed burns favor fire-tolerant regimes such as longleaf pine and wire grass, habitat preferred by the endangered red-cockaded woodpecker.

RAYMOND GEHMAN (ABOVE AND OPPOSITE)

EMORY KRISTOF; RAYMOND GEHMAN (FOLLOWING PAGES)

The Future
195

Notes on Contributors

Author **Kenneth Brower** was born in San Francisco in 1944. He has written about nature, ecology, and wilderness in a number of books, including *The Starship and the Canoe*, *Wake of the Whale*, *A Song for Satawal*, and, for the National Geographic Society, *Yosemite: An American Treasure* and *Realms of the Sea*. Currently at work on a book about tropical rain forest, he lives in Oakland, California, with his two children.

Originally from South Carolina, featured photographer **Raymond Gehman** lives in Pennsylvania's Cumberland Valley with his wife and two sons. His recent work includes two stories for NATIONAL GEOGRAPHIC, on fire ecology and on Banff National Park. He also was principal photographer for two Society books, *Exploring Canada's Spectacular National Parks* and *Yellowstone Country: The Enduring Wonder*.

Acknowledgments

The Book Division wishes to express its gratitude to the men and women of the Forest Service, U.S. Department of Agriculture, for their cooperation and assistance during the preparation of this book. We also thank the individuals and organizations mentioned in the text, as well as those cited here, for their help: Caroline Alkire, Steve Ambrose, Guy Anglin, Lamar Beasley, Erik Berg, Lyn Clement, Andrew Colaninno, Don Collins, Kent Fuellenbach, John Gong, Michael Gryson, Jane Hendron, Chris Holmes, Bob Hoverson, Sherry Hughes, Bill Kaage, Judy Kissinger, Thomas Knappenberger, John Kramer, John Louth, John Nobles, Suzanne Olson, Scott Parsons, Jim Payne, Brian Poturalski, Ken Rinehart, Jim Ruhl, Christopher Shaw, Mike Skinner, Kate Snow, Andy Stahl, Doug Stockdale, Carl Summers, Mark Vanevery, Lizzette Velez, and Dick Zechentmayer.

Additional Reading

Readers may wish to consult the *National Geographic Index* for related articles and books. The following titles may also be of interest: American Birding Association, *Birdfinding in Forty National Forests and Grasslands*; Janine M. Benyus, *Northwoods Wildlife*; David Brower, *For Earth's Sake: The Life and Times of David Brower*; Michael Frome, *Whose Woods These Are: The Story of the National Forests*; Robert G. Ketchum and Carey D. Ketchum, *The Tongass*; Ruth Kirk with Jerry Franklin, *The Olympic Rain Forest*; Oliver LaFarge, *A Pictorial History of the American Indian*; Elbert Little, *The Audubon Society Field Guide to North American Trees*; Robert H. Mohlenbrock, *The Field Guide to U.S. National Forests*; Donald C. Peattie, *A Natural History of Western Trees* and *Natural History of Trees*; John Perlin, *A Forest Journey*; Alfred Runte, *Public Lands, Public Heritage: The National Forest Idea*; Harold K. Steen, *The U. S. Forest Service: A History*; Laurence Walker, *The Southern Forest*; Dyan Zaslowsky and The Wilderness Society, *These American Lands*; and Charles I. Zinser, *Outdoor Recreation*.

Library of Congress ℂℙ Data

Brower, Kenneth, 1944-
      American legacy : our national forests / by Kenneth Brower;
  prepared by the Book Division, National Geographic Society.
      p. cm.
      Includes bibliographical references and index.
      ISBN 0-7922-3650-5 (reg.). — ISBN 0-7922-4230-0 (dlx.)
      1. Forest reserves—United States.   I. National Geographic Society
  (U.S.).   Book Division. II. Title.
  SD426.B66   1997
  333.75'16'097—dc21   96—37341
                                          ℂℙ

Composition for this book by the National Geographic Society Book Division. Printed and bound by R. R. Donnelley & Sons, Willard, Ohio. Color separations by CMI Color Graphix, Inc., Huntingdon Valley, Pa.; Phototype Color Graphics, Pennsauken, N.J.; Digital Color Image, Pennsauken, N.J.; Graphic Art Service, Inc., Nashville, Tenn. Dust jacket printed by Miken Companies, Inc., Cheektowaga, N.Y.

Visit the Society's Web site at **http://www.nationalgeographic.com.**